Gordon of Khartoum

To my son, DOMINIC

Gordon of Khartoum

Patrick Turnbull

BAILEY BROTHERS & SWINFEN LIMITED
FOLKESTONE

Published in Great Britain by
Bailey Brothers and Swinfen Ltd.

SBN 561 00232 0

Printed in Great Britain by
Whitstable Litho Ltd., Whitstable, Kent.

Contents

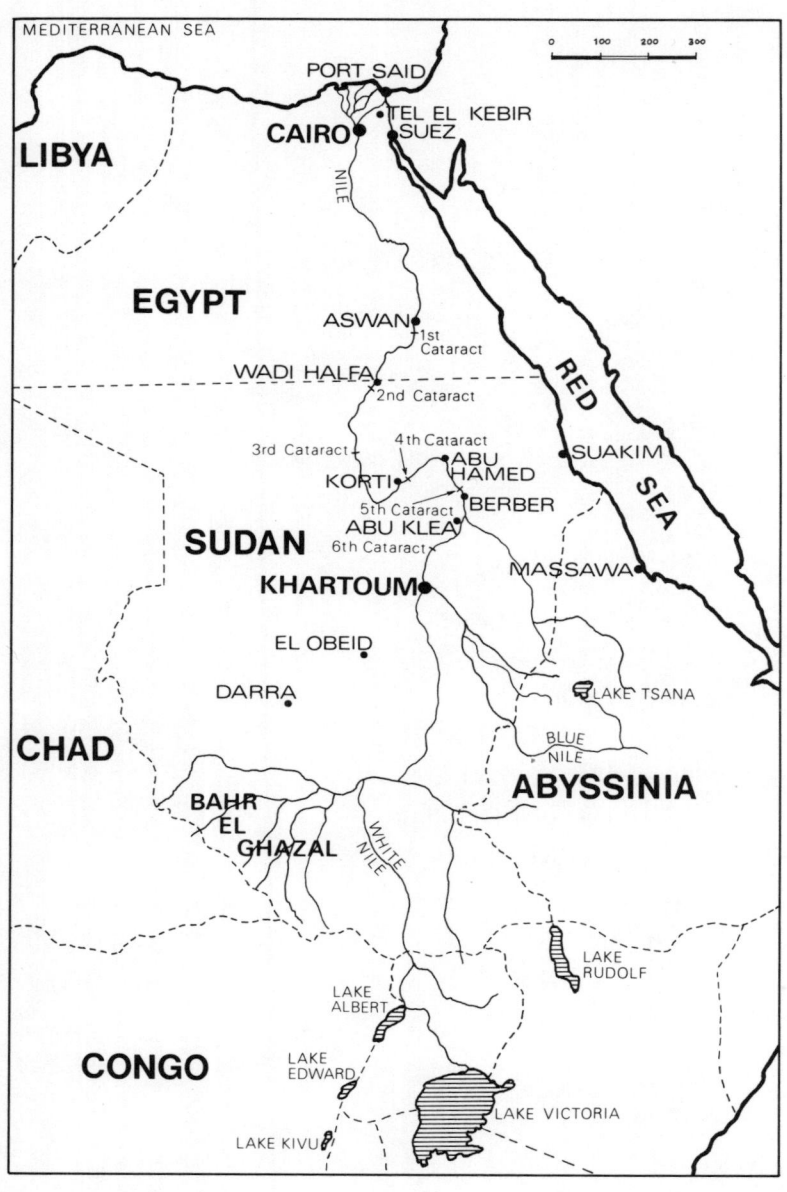

1

The Birth of a Legend

In the early 1840s the inhabitants of Woolwich, and especially the staff of the Royal Military Academy, were constantly in fear of having their windows broken by metal screws and other blunt objects, hurtled through the air by an unknown hand. 'Unknown' should, perhaps, be qualified by the word 'officially', for it was suspected, and in this case suspicions were well founded, that the authors of these disturbances were none other than the children of the Inspector of the Carriage Department of the R.M.A., Colonel Gordon, led by one of his younger sons — of a family of eleven — Charles George, born January 28, 1833.

Although Colonel Gordon was a straightlaced traditionalist, proud of being descended from a long line of Highland warriors, and his wife, Elizabeth, daughter of a wealthy shipowner, forbiddingly, puritanically, austere, at an early age Charles George became known as one of the most mischievous, reckless, rebellious-minded youngsters of the neighbourhood. Yet equally early in life, he gave evidence of

1

latent genius only waiting for the right acquaintances, the right circumstances, to be developed; a genius orientated inevitably to the military furrow.

As a child he loved playing with his huge army of toy soldiers, reading any book, no matter how abstruse, on military matters, map drawing, and, from the practical point of view, organising his elder brothers in thrilling window smashing escapades, alternating with the less damaging prank of ringing front door bells, then disappearing before the door could be opened. What does seem strange is that in such an age of iron discipline for the young, these outbursts of high spirits went unpunished; undoubtedly the goddess Fortune who took such care of the young Charles throughout his campaigns when, as so often happened, he gave the impression of courting death, saved him from many a severe beating inevitable had such exploits been *officially* exposed.

It never occurred to Charles that he would take up any other career than the army. On leaving Taunton school in 1847, he entered the R.M.A. grounds, not as a tentative window smasher, but as a cadet, displaying unusual brilliance for his age. It has been recorded that 'his drawings of guns and forts stand to this day as model examples in the Royal School of Military Engineering'. He had every possibility of passing out top of his year, but, unfortunately for his future, he was a born rebel unable to submit to the norm of discipline demanded by the Academy.

He was soon at loggerheads with his seniors. On one occasion the juniors had been told not to leave the dining hall, and the only exit — leading to a staircase — was blocked by the senior cadet corporal. The sight of this symbol of repression, arms outstretched, was more than Gordon could bear. He charged, head lowered. Before the flabbergasted corporal realised what was happening or had time to dodge, Gordon's head caught him full in the stomach, sending him crashing over backwards down the flight of stairs and through a glass door.

As a senior, he was equally irascible. His record shows

that he was had up before the Commandant during his last term, and reprimanded for beating a junior over the head with a hair brush. Worse still he was always prepared to argue technical points with his instructors. As a result of these various misdemeanours, on passing out he found himself gazetted, much to his disappointment, not to the Royal Artillery, but to the Royal Engineers, looked upon as a refuge for the military eccentric and whose officers were reputed to be, in popular military parlance – 'mad, married, or methodist.'

Commissioned at the age of 19, he was first posted to the Royal Engineer Depot, Chatham, then eighteen months later to Pembroke Dock, Wales. From the beginning, he worked so hard that his Academy escapades were either forgotten or dismissed as the outcome of youthful exuberance, but while at Pembroke Dock he was stricken for the first time by what was to become with him a form of disease; boredom.

One of Charles Gordon's youthful handicaps was that his looks totally belied his character. There was nothing tough about his appearance. He was slenderly built, and had grey-blue eyes, a voice so soft that it was difficult to make out what he was saying, and a shy, rather hesitant manner. He was the sort of young subaltern senior officers' wives either wanted to mother, or considered as the ideal husband for one of their daughters as he was obviously far too 'nice' – so they imagined – ever to be mixed up in intrigue; regimental, political, or extra-marital.

Their calculations could not have been more erroneous. The mild-eyed young subaltern appealing so strongly to their maternal instincts was a social bear. He detested dancing, organised social games such as tennis, tea and dinner parties. In fact he had no interests outside the purely military aspect of life, and was far too ambitious to allow himself to be caught up in matrimony's mesh. Except when to do so would have caused positive harm to his career, he consistently refused all invitations.

3

The only impact made on him at Pembroke was by an older social rebel, Captain Drew, a man deeply religious, but eccentrically non-conformist who insisted that though he belonged to no recognized church, he was a better Christian than the majority of regular church goers.

From his mother Gordon had inherited a natural wish to 'believe' combined with a marked tendency to mysticism. But as a boy his equally natural aversion to discipline had turned him against the established church to such a degree that, indifferent to the scandal caused, he refused categorically to be confirmed. Rather like the Frenchman Charles de Foucauld some thirty years later, once a 'believer' — as indeed he became after long conversations and arguments with Captain Drew — his enthusiasm at having discovered 'God and the Truth' dominated his thoughts and actions to a very large extent for the rest of his life. And again like de Foucauld, one sees as a result of this 'conversion' the birth of a death wish, developing over the years into a gnawing longing for martyrdom. Furthermore this death wish seems to have supplanted in his nature any attraction which he might normally have felt for the opposite sex. Never at any time throughout his varied career was there the least hint of romance. Instead he made his eldest sister, Augusta, ten years his senior and a humourless bigot, his confidante and confessor, bombarding her almost till the day of his death with interminable letters, laying bare his soul, pouring out his hopes, his fears, his most secret thoughts and ambitions.

Thanks to Captain Drew, Gordon had become so deeply immersed in the unfathomable ocean of 'Faith', that he might well have left the service but for the outbreak of the Crimean War which, without in any way dimming his religious fervour, nevertheless re-awoke those military instincts which had been so much part of him since birth.

It may also have helped that Gordon was able to persuade himself that this obscure, senseless, conflict could have been described as a 'religious war' since its origin stemmed from rival claims as to who was to administer Jerusalem's Holy Places, even though the final line-up found Christian Russia opposed to Christian France and Britain allied to Moslem Turkey. The true reasons for the outbreak of hostilities were indeed purely political. Russia's claim to control in Jerusalem was merely an excuse to secure a springboard for western expansion. Britain and France, allies for the first time in history, were resolutely determined to frustrate all Russian attempts to become a Mediterranean power. While Turkey, well in her decline, lay caught up, a buffer state, near helpless victim between the two 'spheres of influence'.

As the British army had not been involved in a major war since Waterloo, there were very few officers, especially junior officers, who were not delighted at the chance to prove their worth in battle and win quick promotion, at the same time escaping from the deadly dull routine of garrison life. All over the country Russophobia erupted as Tennyson, the poet laureate, declaimed against the 'o'ergrown Barbarian of the East.'

Charles Gordon, in common with most of his brother officers, fell victim to war fever, aggravated when his brother Henry sailed with his infantry battalion with the first convoy to the Black Sea. Then, to his intense annoyance, weeks merged into months and still no posting order was received, other than to Corfu, considered a complete backwater, which he was fortunate enough to have cancelled. To add to his despair, despatches from the Crimea splashed in the press were giving vivid, if at times slightly prejudiced, accounts of 'victories' at the Alma, Inkermann and Balaclava, and the subsequent investment of Sebastopol. Others, he fretted, were winning awards and promotion while his only battle was dodging social engagements. Finally, he called at the War Office asking for an interview with General Sir John Burgoyne, Inspector General of Fortifications, hoping that this old friend of his father's would be able to pull the necessary strings. In the mid nineteenth century influence still counted. The result of this visit to Whitehall materialised in the form of a posting order to British Army HQ in the Crimea in December.

Gordon reached his destination on the bleak winter afternoon of New Year's Day 1855, his mind torn between professional longing to distinguish himself in action and a mystical yearning to make the supreme sacrifice. Many years later, just before his last journey to the Sudan, he wrote to Augusta — 'I went to the Crimea hoping without having a hand in it to be killed. . .', while several letters from the Front told his readers that he was 'prepared for death'. From start to finish of the campaign his behaviour under fire seems to confirm this statement, and his determination to do everything the hardest way.

Outside Sebastopol, during the misery of a Russian winter, when mere survival under such trying conditions degenerated into a battle with the elements, irrespective of the human enemy, Gordon turned his back on the few comforts available; minor comforts which the majority of his brother officers considered necessities to enable them to face the ordeals of daily existence: bitter cold, snow storms, drenching rain, fevers, debilitation. And though only in his early twenties, an age when most young officers were either too much in awe of, or too discreet, to criticise those on the upper steps of the hierarchy, from the moment of his arrival with the Expeditionary Force, he was virulent in his attacks on the privileges of senior officers who enjoyed comforts not available to the 'troops'; such indulgence, since it was they who should be setting an example in hard living, he described as 'iniquitous'. At the same time, with strange perversity, he showed a marked lack of sympathy with the 'other ranks' for making no efforts to better their miserable condition. 'They are like children' he accused, 'thinking everything should be done for them.'

He was equally critical of the French. Their army, he said

'talked a great deal' but 'their courage was found wanting by comparison with their Russian enemies'.

Although his carping attitude earned him many angry comments, nobody could accuse him of not practising what he preached. He was always volunteering for dangerous jobs. Solitary reconaissances in the no-man's-land between British and Russian lines held a particular appeal for him. Senior officers who resented his manner still had to admit that no one was calmer when bullets were whizzing round. Only once did his apparent invulnerability let him down. He was slightly wounded when a shell killed the man standing next to him, but was back in the line within ten days, anxious to be sent on further missions.

The aftermath of war, the time for the distribution of awards, called forth more adverse criticisms, even though Gordon himself had no reason to complain. He received the British war medal, the Turkish war medal, and France's *Légion d'Honneur.* But this did not prevent him from writing scornfully to Augusta about the 'shower of decorations and promotions which fell upon senior officers' and the 'easily earned C.Bs and majorities there have been in some cases', and as verbal discretion was not part of his make-up, the sarcasms which he dispensed not only on paper but in the course of conversations in the mess, probably contributed to the fact that once the war was ended, instead of returning to England as one of the conquering heroes, he was posted to Bessarabia on a frontier commission. It might even have been suggested by incensed senior officers that he was more fitted for civilian life. But in those months outside Sebastopol, he had shown himself to be an inspired soldier, and had already laid the foundations of that legend of personal courage which stayed with him all his life. 'Time and again he would expose himself quite unnecessarily to enemy fire' one citation read 'unarmed and without an escort, carrying out reconaissances of the Russian fortifications, supervising the digging of rifle pits, far in advance of the front line trenches, and only a few yards from the Russian picket lines.' In fact it is no exaggeration to say that it was little short of a miracle that he lived to see the white flag raised above Sebastopol.

During the campaign he earned the admiration of a Lieutenant — future field marshal — Wolseley, better known as Sir Garnet, later Lord, Wolseley, who wrote home that he 'was most impressed by young Gordon's full, clear and bright eyes, and indifference to danger of all sorts' adding that he himself felt in comparison 'inferior in all the higher qualities of character' and ending 'and how inferior all my aims in life are to his. . .'

It was not until 1858, nearly four years after leaving England, that Gordon returned to the British Isles. They had been intensely formative years. In the wilds of Armenia, Bessarabia, the Caucasus, he had become imbued with a love of the 'wide open spaces', of the primitive life, a love running parallel with an increasing horror of the ways of conventional western civilization. There were no regrets at staying in the Balkans while others sailed for home. 'I expect I shall remain abroad' he wrote to Augusta 'for three or four years which, *individually,* I would sooner spend in war than peace. There is something indescribably exciting in the former. . .'

He was never to lose his distaste for 'normal' life — probably another reason for remaining single — so it was not surprising that as soon as he set foot on English soil he wrote to his parents 'I do not feel at all inclined to settle in England and be employed in a sedentary way', or that promotion to captain failed to stifle his wanderlust. Routine at Chatham, where he was posted for the second time, became so irksome that although he was depot adjutant, in 1860 he volunteered for service in China, where Britain and the Chinese Emperor were on the brink of war over the latter's refusal to ratify the Treaty of Tientsin.

The struggle with China as a nation had been almost resolved before Gordon reached the Far East. The chain of events which brought him world fame and the title 'Chinese Gordon' was for the most part interwoven not in a conflict involving China with Queen Victoria's England, but in that of the Chinese Emperor with a rebellious subject, Hung Hsiu Chuan, whose object was nothing less than the overthrow of the Pekin Manchu dynasty, and the proclamation of Christianity as the offical state religion.

Hung Hsiu Chuan was a southern Chinese, son of the headman of the Hung clan of the Hakka tribe, a race which had never been reconciled to the defeat of the ancient Ming dynasty by the 'barbarian' Tartar Manchus some two hundred years previously. Though his conversion to Christianity as a result of being educated by Baptist missionaries had taken on an unusually militant form, he was, like the man eventually responsible for his downfall, something of a mystic.

As a young man he had nearly died of a virulent bout of fever.

During his illness, when his life was despaired, Hung claimed to have actually passed over from the land of the living to the spirit world where he was confronted by 'The Venerable in Years' and ordered to return to earth to serve His purpose since 'You are my son'. The fever passed miraculously, and as soon as he was on his feet again, Hung let it be known that he was the 'Chosen of God', born to destroy the corrupt Manchu dynasty, and proceeded to issue proclamations setting forth 'the noble principles of the Heavenly King, Hung Hsiu Chuan' written in red ink, till then the prerogative of the reigning family. His subversive activities were helped by the Manchu Emperor's humiliating defeat in what is generally known as the 'Opium War' resulting in the handing over of Hong Kong to Britain, and the establishment of European 'concessions' in Shanghai and other trading centres.

His attempts to persuade the Baptist missionaries responsible for his conversion that he was of divine origin

9

were not successful. They dismissed him as a lunatic. Their rejection did not worry him. *He* was right, the 'foreigners' wrong. Confident in his own powers, he set off on a tour of southern China, to bring the locals into the fold, in his highly individual interpretation of Christianity describing the Trinity as 'God the Father, Christ the son and elder brother, and Hung the other son of God and Christ's younger brother.' A confirmed iconoclast, his path was marked by the ruins of temples. His violence was so terrifying that even the most famous of the dreaded secret societies were cowed into supporting him, including the most powerful of all, the Triad — the 'Heaven and Earth Society' — led by an unfrocked Buddhist priest, Chu.

In January 1851, Hung felt that he had gained enough power to issue his first 'Order of the Day', in which he insisted that he was the Supreme Leader, that any order emanating from him must be obeyed blindly and unquestioningly, at the same time reminding his followers that their lives must be based on the tenets set forth by the Ten Commandments. He then announced that he was the Tien Wang (the Heavenly King) and leader of the movement which he styled the Taiping Tien-Kuo, or Heavenly Kingdom of Great Peace, following this proclamation by issuing the formal order to march on Pekin, some two thousand miles distant, and kick the usurper Manchu from his throne.

The army which he gathered together was modelled on exaggerated Cromwellian lines, puritanism marching hand in glove with brutal discipline. Admirably, all the normal vices of Chinese armies of that time were suppressed; bribery, opium smoking, prostitution. But Hung was in such a state of religious exaltation that he let it be known that at times God came down from Heaven to talk to him, and to ensure that his men were worthy of so holy a leader, went as far as to make it a rule that any recruit who within three weeks of becoming one of the Tien Wang's soldiers, failed to learn the Lord's Prayer and the Ten Commandments, would be executed. In spite of such Draconian methods the men shared their leader's fervour for the cause to such an extent that, by April 1852, Hung's armies, commanded in the field by Li Siu Cheng, a man of unusual military talent, generally known as the Chung Wang (the Faithful King), after inflicting a number of defeats on the Manchu forces, had reached the Yangtze valley. These victories were quickly exploited by the capture of the cities of Wuchang and Hangkow.

However, after so many disasters, the Imperialists were lucky enough to find a leader of rare integrity and talent, Tseng Kuo Fan, whose counter 'model army' was able to halt Hung's advance on the capital. After this first check to his forces, Hung broke off the operation to march rapidly on Nanking which fell after only very feeble resistance. On breaking into the city, the Taipings, as they were now generally known, murdered some 28,000 men, women, and children in cold blood. Encouraged by this success, Hung ordered another attack on Pekin, but by then the imperialists had been reinforced by a Mongolian contingent. The Taipings were cut to pieces and were never again able to threaten the capital, but undaunted Hung continued to mop up isolated Manchu garrisons, and eventually appeared outside both Hong Kong and Shanghai.

Sir George Bonham, Governor of Hong Kong, demanded an interview with Hung who insisted that he must always be addressed as the Tien Wang, and who, despite the Pekin setbacks, had lost none of his fanatical megalomania. The interview was stormy. The Tien Wang maintained that all foreigners in China were his subjects. Sir George reminded him that as far as Britain was concerned the Manchus were China's legal sovereigns. Feeling that Hong Kong was too formidable an obstacle to tackle, Hung withdrew angrily and marched to Shanghai.

In threatening European interests, Hung made a fatal mistake. Till then his professed — even though exotic — Christianity had won him considerable favour in Europe, but his attacks on Christian purses effectively alienated such latent sympathy.

In 1857, however, it looked as if the Tien Wang's popularity might be enhanced as a result of a further clash between Britain and France and the Pekin Governement, and a brief campaign during which Canton was seized by a mixed British/Indian and French force. The aftermath of this campaign, however, was totally contrary to the Tien Wang's expectations. Under duress the Emperor signed a 'Treaty of peace and friendship' with Britain and France acknowledging the latters' right to trade up the Yangtze river as far as Hankow 'as soon as peace presently disturbed by outlaws shall have been restored'. There could be no doubt at whom this clause was aimed, and for the Tien Wang it was a shattering blow.

All through the long journey, Gordon had been worrying that he would 'miss the fun', but when he disembarked at Shanghai on September 7, the country was still in a state of upheaval. Shanghai itself was threatened by Hung's Taipings, while a punitive expedition was about to be despatched to Pekin to punish the Emperor — officially an ally — for imperialist inspired attacks on British shipping.

To his delight, Gordon was attached to this expedition which reached the Imperial city on October 6. The British were in an angry mood. Envoys who had entered Pekin under a flag of truce to try to arrange a settlement had been seized, and though some were released after being brutally treated, others were held and tortured.

'Poor de Norman who was with me in Asia' Gordon wrote 'was one of the victims. It appears they were tied so tightly by the wrists that the flesh mortified and they died in the greatest agony. . .' While one of the survivors, Sir Henry Parkes, stated 'they (the prisoners) were exposed in an open court for three days and nights, very little food and water given them, but blows in abundance. Delirium set in in some cases. . .'

Lord Elgin, directing British policy, decided that the Chinese must be taught a lesson. Orders were, therefore, given, that the Imperial Palace which stood outside the city walls was to be razed to the ground, and it was to Gordon that this unusual work of demolition was entrusted.

It was not a task to his liking. He described it as 'wretchedly demoralizing' and went on to say that 'in this Tartar Emperor's mansion there is as much splendour and civilization as you would see at Windsor . . . you can scarcely imagine the beauty and the magnificence of the places we burnt. It made one's heart sore to burn them. . .' Yet believing as he did in doing a job thoroughly, by the time he had finished the Palace was nothing but a smoking heap of rubble.

When they finally withdrew from Pekin, the British left a force some 3,000 strong at Tientsin 'just to keep an eye on the Emperor', under the command of General Staveley, whose sister had married one of Gordon's elder brothers. Gordon remained with this garrison, but spent most of his time making long excursions into the interior, including a reconnaissance of the Great Wall of China, then an area almost unknown, and officially forbidden to Europeans. Recalled to Shanghai in May 1862, he was employed on the improvement of the city's defences, rather bored and craving further action.

His chance to escape from the rut occurred unexpectedly in January 1863.

Shanghai had become of such importance to both British and French business interests, that it had been decided to strengthen the regular garrison by raising and paying an auxiliary corps, recruited from the riff-raff haunting the docks; a sort of foreign legion entrusted to the command of an American, Frederic Townsend Ward. After falling foul of the authorities when it was found that he was persuading French and British sailors to desert with the promise of high pay and golden opportunities to loot, Ward's force was re-organized with European officers, but exclusively Chinese other ranks. Calling this strange corps The Ever Victorious Army, Ward and his second-in-command, another American of French origin, Burgevine, won three battles in rapid succession against the Taipings. But in September (1862) Ward was killed, and command passed automatically to Burgevine who was soon at loggerheads with both the British authorities and the local Chinese Governor, Li Hung Chang.

Suffering the after effects of a wound received in the same battle in which Ward had been killed, Burgevine kept the Ever Victorious Army in barracks and refused an order to attack a Taiping outpost. To punish this disobedience, Governor Li stated that no more pay would be issued. Knowing that such a measure could well provoke a mutiny with his mercenaries, Burgevine swore that he would collect the money himself. With a small escort, he descended on the house of the banker Ta Kee and demanded that the money be handed over the counter immediately. When Ta Kee refused, Burgevine knocked him down, and helped himself to the money; 40,000 dollars.

Li was shrewd enough to realise that the Ever Victorious Army could be considered a major factor in the preservation of Shanghai from the Tien Wang's depredations, but at the same time could not afford to lose face by ignoring the affront. Acting in agreement with the European authorities, he formally dismissed Burgevine from his command replacing him by General Staveley's chief of staff, Captain Holland of the Royal Marines, who was ordered to take the offensive immediately. As Holland was given no time to prepare a proper plan or even issue adequate operation orders, the take-over, not surprisingly, proved disastrous.

The action was described by one of the Taiping leaders — 'Oh how we laughed the morning of the assault, as they (Holland's men) advanced nearer to the creek which they had brought no bridges to throw over. "What a General he is," cried our chief "who sends his men to storm a city without first ascertaining there is a moat!" So we laughed and we jested as we saw the slaves of the Tartar usurper marching to destruction. . .'

The result of this complete loss of 'face' was the proposed relief of Holland and his replacement by Gordon, the suggestion being put forward by General Staveley and approved, though only after second thoughts, by Sir Frederick Bruce, British Minister in Pekin, who had heard and disapproved of Gordon's slightly eccentric behaviour. Gordon knew of this and was not expecting the appointment to be confirmed. He was all the more pleased, therefore, when on March 26, he was promoted brevet-major to become official commander of the Ever Victorious Army.

The title 'Army' was very much of an exaggeration. Gordon's command consisted of a mere 3,500 men; a mixed force of infantry and artillery. Although by then the other ranks were all Chinese, the officers were a truly international band. There were Americans, French, Spaniards, Germans, Swedes, and 'misfits from all the countries of the United Kingdom'. Discipline in the field was harsh, but at the same time it was looked upon as a mercenary's privilege to loot, and to haunt gambling and vice dens when in barracks.

Stern puritan, Gordon was not prepared to tolerate any form of moral laxity at any time. He was not willing even to compromise. Discipline, he stressed, would be as tight in rest periods as on the battlefield. Lapses could even be punishable by death. This 'new look' was as unpopular with the officers as with the men. But Gordon was not a man to listen to sophistry. The Ever Victorious Army would, from then on, be modelled to his pattern. In the subsequent clash of wills, Gordon was obliged to suppress two mutinies, and admit the loss of a good third of his men from desertion.

Undaunted he set about reorganizing his force. Deserters were replaced by recruits attracted by high pay, and above all by the fact that pay was guaranteed. At the same time he concentrated on battle training and the morale factor, confident that his men, well armed — he was adamant on this question — and masters of the tactics he himself had evolved, would be so imbued with a sense of superiority, especially in a country where morale, as he had seen for himself, was of supreme importance, that they would prove worthy of the title of the 'army' in which they were serving.

Li and the commander of the imperial forces in the area, General Ching, an ex-Taiping, had the good sense to give Gordon their total backing, and though basically xenophobe, Li conceived a grudging affection for Gordon as a man, going as far as to call him a 'direct blessing from Heaven' and noting 'He is superior in manner and bearing to any of the foreigners I have come across and does not show outwardly that conceit which makes most of them repugnant in my sight. Besides which he is possessed of a splendid military bearing and is direct and business like.'

This confidence soon proved justified when, led in person by Gordon, the Ever Victorious Army raised the siege of Chanzu on the Yangtze estuary against a vastly superior enemy, a victory which won him the Order of the Yellow Button and the rank of General of Division of the Chinese Army.

Gordon's tactics, which enabled him to win this success, served as a basic pattern for future operations.

Although light field artillery was included in the Ever Victorious Army, he had two heavy 32 pounder guns mounted on a river steamer, the *Hyson,* which he also used as his Headquarters, the *Hyson* always being accompanied by a second steamer with a strong detachment of infantry aboard, the two vessels constituting a mobile striking force.

It was the *Hyson's* heavy guns which had driven the Taipings from Fushan, a fort protecting the approaches to Chanzu, while panic at the news of the devastating bombardment to which Fushan had been submitted had made the defenders of the stockades erected along the river banks take to their heels before putting up any serious resistance. In ten days, with only trifling losses, the whole operation had been successfully concluded, and the Ever Victorious Army was back at Sunkiang where Gordon at once got down to the task of instilling further discipline into his still independent-minded troops.

This success came at an opportune moment, for Burgevine had been trying to pull strings to get himself reinstated. In these attempts it is rather astonishing to find that he was supported by Sir Frederick Bruce, who went as far as to say that, in his opinion, Li's dismissal of Burgevine was un-justified. Li, however, was not prepared to give in. Knowing that the British authorities in Shanghai supported him, he sent an urgent message to Pekin, urging that rather than be dismissed Gordon should be promoted to the rank of Tsung Ping, or General of Division, a request granted immediately.

Gordon's next feat more than justified this promotion.

The walled town of Taitsan had been the scene of Holland's defeat, a defeat which Gordon was burning to avenge not only as an insult to the Ever Victorious Army's prestige, but to that of Britain. Embarking his whole force of about 3,000 on a flotilla of river steamers, he appeared unexpectedly before the stockades guarding the town's main gates which were seized by a storming party after a brief but severe bombardment. As easy a victory as had been won at Chanzu seemed possible but the defenders' morale was high after the Holland disaster. Though the walls were soon breached by the *Hyson's* guns, once within the town the attackers came up against determined resistance.

Twice the assaulting troops were thrown back.

It was then that Gordon, armed only with a light ratan cane, led a third charge, setting an example of reckless courage which proved the deciding factor. To quote his own words — 'The rebels made a good fight but it was no use and the place fell. . .', and in a letter to his mother, hastily scribbled in pencil, 'I have just taken Taitsan without much

17

loss (not strictly speaking correct; over 300 of his men had been killed) and am, thanks to Providence, untouched'. He was less laconic in a letter to a fellow officer, saying 'It really was a tremendous fight and I never hope to see another like it', and talking of the Chinese as soldiers, he commented 'Their bravery is passive, but in some cases would outdo even foreign bravery.'

Li was delighted, though his army commander, Ching, had great difficulty in restraining his jealousy, a sentiment which did not make for harmony when a couple of days later the Ever Victorious Army reached the outskirts of Quinsan, another Taiping stronghold. Li's plan was that Gordon and Ching should join forces for a combined attack on the town, but the two men quarrelled as soon as they met.

Ching wished Gordon to attack immediately. Gordon refused to undertake another operation till his men had been back to Sunkiang to refit and replace casualties. Despite Ching's protests, Gordon continued to Sunkiang where he had to squash an embryo mutiny of malcontents furious at not having been allowed to pillage Taitsan. After he had shown that he was just as capable of dealing with insubordination as with an enemy fortress, Gordon was back with Ching outside Quinsan on May 28.

The attack was launched two days later, the Ever Victorious Army in the van, Ching making sure that his own force was so far in reserve that it was never seriously engaged. Resistance was less ferocious than at Taitsan, collapsing in less than twenty four hours, but that evening there occurred an incident which, unjustly, earned Gordon considerable adverse criticism both in Shanghai and in England.

Shots were still being exchanged when, in the darkness, he noticed 'a confused mass crowding along near a high bridge on the northern bank'. This in fact was the major part of Quinsan's garrison, some 8,000 strong, attempting to escape under cover of night. 'Matters were in too critical a state' Gordon wrote later 'to hesitate, as the mass of rebels, goaded into desperation, would have swept our small force away. We were, therefore, forced to fire on them.'

Taiping casualties were enormous. There was a *sauve qui peut*. By morning over fifteen hundred corpses littered the escape route. But, as Gordon pointed out, had the enemy tried to hold out, their casualties would inevitably have been considerably higher. This did not prevent him from being accused of having organized a massacre by continuing his 'murderous fire' for an unnecessarily long time.

Always worried by the fact that the Taipings were, after all, fellow Christians, Gordon was deeply hurt and worried by these attacks. In fact the period following the Quinsan victory was for him one of very great stress and frustration. There were further violent quarrels with the jealous Ching, and Li noted 'Ching threatens to resign if some curb is not put upon General Gordon. Ching is far from being a great military man, but he has a quick temper like Gordon, and they are both ready to say hot words, like myself. . .' Matters came to such a pitch that in June, Ching's troops opened fire and killed two of Gordon's men. But for the fact that Ching was frightened into making the most abject apology, the so-called allies might have been involved in an all-out battle.

Then there was trouble with his own men.

Having decided that Sungkiang's opium dens and other night haunts were highly injurious to the morale and combat capability of a fighting force, he had made up his mind to move, lock, stock and barrel, to Quinsan. It was a decision which sparked off a veritable explosion of protests and acts of open defiance. The would-be mutineers had chosen their moment badly. Because of attacks on him in the press and continual bickering with Li, Gordon was in an angry mood. The whole of the Ever Victorious Army was paraded, the mutineers threatened by the bayonets of those who had remained loyal. An artillery corporal, known to be a ringleader, was dragged from the ranks and shot on the spot. When it was announced that if the other ringleaders were not named immediately every fifth man would suffer a similar fate, the guilty ones were promptly betrayed. There were no more protests or acts of defiance.

But hardly had this mutiny been crushed than there was trouble with Li. Possibly because he wished to pacify Ching, Li began to hold up the Ever Victorious Army's pay and to delay supplies of ammunition and equipment. When Gordon complained, his complaints were ignored. In a rage, he wrote to Li resigning his command which he declared to be 'derogatory to my position as a British officer who cannot be a suppliant for what Your Excellency knows to be necessities and should be happy to give. . .'

This was the first of a long series of resignations, made in anger and on the spur of the moment, which were to mark the entire path of his astonishing career.

Although only in his early thirties, Charles George Gordon was already very much in the public eye. He had proved himself to be a soldier of genius, combining an exceptional fearlessness under fire with a tactical flair and gift for leadership which had ensured him victory. Yet the chinks in his armour had also been revealed; inability to ride criticism, a childish petulance were his will opposed, translating itself increasingly with the years by resignation quickly to be followed by cancellation of that same resignation. But one truth was already manifest from the maze of moral and psychological contradictions; he was a fanatic. Nothing was capable of diverting him from a chosen path. And this fanaticism was not merely religious; it permeated each and every one of his actions, from the most insignificant to those which in their evolution were to effect, in some degree, world history.

2

Chinese Gordon

His moment of blind anger past, Gordon began to sum up the situation coldly.

The Ever Victorious Army was in a sorry state, and this reflected adversely on his pride. It was *his* army, and he could not abandon it at such a moment. 'I am the only stay of the force' he wrote to Augusta 'and on my life hangs its existence.' He was certain that his continued presence alone could prevent the rot.

Governor Li, for his part, pretended to ignore all knowledge of Gordon's letter, especially as his next objective was the capture of the Taiping citadel of Soochow, second only in importance to the 'Heavenly' capital, Nanking, in which he counted on the Ever Victorious Army again leading the assault.

Gordon was not deceived by Li's apparent tact, but as he could not bear the thought of his men marching without him, the matter was dropped.

Though his death wish was still with him, so that he

welcomed further opportunities of courting the killer bullet, Gordon had begun to take a pride in winning a victory with the smallest possible loss to his own force. With this in mind, he based his plans for the coming campaign on the fire power of the *Hyson,* and other similarly armed steamers, holding back his infantry till the defence had been so softened up, that a minimum resistance was likely to be offered to the final assault.

Nevertheless, as Ching's imperial regiments and the Ever Victorious Army advanced on Soochow, there were a number of sharp engagements round the series of stockades barring the way. As usual it was Gordon who led every charge, still with no other weapon than his ratan cane which his men were now convinced was a magic, life-preserving, wand. His luck held. He was not even scratched, though at Leiku village he owed his survival to a young American officer, Captain Perry.

It was a strange story. For some unknown reason Perry had passed information concerning imperial plans to the Taipings. One of these letters was intercepted, and Gordon would have been quite justified in ordering Perry to be executed. Instead he preferred to give him a chance to 'redeem himself' by occupying the place of greatest danger from then on.

'Opportunity soon came (at Leiku). The rebel fire was accurate and heavy. Gordon crouched with his men in a ditch, beside him was Perry. Gordon told him that his time had come and to lead the charge. Perry did so. But even in such a case, Gordon could not send any man where he himself would not go. So Gordon was beside him as he dashed forward. Perry managed to get ahead of his commander, and there received a bullet which otherwise would have struck Gordon himself. Perry fell into the arms of the man he had betrayed. There he died. Gordon's laconic comment was that Perry "was such an owlet that it (the betrayal) made no difference" '.

In mid-October, the ring round Soochow closed. At this point Li urged Gordon to lead an assault on the city, again with Ching in reserve. Gordon would not agree. So long as Soochow fell, he argued, and fall it must, the odd week, even month, made no difference. And as Ching was equally unwilling to find himself in the van, Li was obliged to play a waiting game.

However, in November, both Ching and Gordon received information from spies that one of the rebel leaders — or Wangs — a certain Lar Wang, hoping to be taken back into the imperial army from which he had deserted to become a follower of the Tien Wang, was trying to persuade the Soochow garrison commander Moh Wang to surrender. His efforts failed. Moh was a fanatical disciple of the Tien Wang. He insisted that they must fight to the end. In early December, he called a meeting of the Soochow notables at which he gave an excellent speech in favour of carrying on the resistance. He had just finished speaking when one of Lar Wang's men crept up behind him and stabbed him nine times in the back. Dragged dying into the street, he was decapitated and his head sent to Ching as a peace offering. Next morning, December 5, the city gates were opened, after Ching had assured Lar Wang's envoy that property would be respected and the lives of the Soochow Wangs spared.

To his horror, Gordon, who had been present when Ching gave his solemn promises to the Wangs' delegate, saw what was to be the beginning of a veritable orgy of looting and arson on the part of the imperial troops as they swarmed through the opened gates, in which his own men were only too anxious to join.

It was another miracle due to force of will that he was able to stop them, collect them together, and, in spite of furious protests march them back to Li's Headquarters, installed on a river steamer near Quinsan. There he demanded a two months' bonus of pay for every man under his command to compensate them for having played 'the major part in the capture of Soochow and for respecting the no-looting order.' Li was obstinate. He said he would agree to a one month bonus but no more. To avoid a further mutiny, Gordon ordered his second-in-command to march the men straight back to Quinsan to await developments. The order was obeyed, but the men were so angry that Gordon took the precaution of standing guard personally over Li's headquarters, a loaded revolver in his hand.

Without another word to Li, he then hurried back to Soochow where he learned that Ching's troops were not only looting but murdering anyone they thought guilty of hiding personal possessions. Through burning streets, Gordon hurried to Lar Wang's palace. Lar was not at home; with the other Wangs he had gone to confer with Li. The rest of his family was huddled, helpless and terrified, in the courtyard, expecting to have their throats cut at any minute. Gathering them together like a flock of sheep, Gordon led them under his personal protection to Lar's uncle's house.

Instead of being thanked by the uncle, he was accused of having betrayed the Wangs, and kept a virtual prisoner for the night, only being released the following morning after giving his promise to go straight to Li and remind him of the terms he had offered.

Waiting for a steamer, he was approached by a group of mounted men. It was Ching with a cavalry escort.

His nerves on edge, Gordon rounded on the General, accusing him of encouraging his men to behave like wild animals, and then demanded news of the Wangs. Apologetic, obviously uneasy, Ching blamed Li for the looting, then said that at the meeting the previous day, the Wangs had behaved in an arrogant and overbearing fashion, refused to sign the surrender, and finally walked out. Having said that, he cut short the conversation and rode away hurriedly, leaving Gordon thoroughly uneasy.

Ching was barely out of sight when a Major Bailey, an American artilleryman who Gordon had lent as adviser to the imperial army, appeared, accompanied by one of Lar's younger sons. The boy confirmed Gordon's fears. All the Wangs, including his father, had been murdered and their bodies were lying exposed to public gaze on the far side of the creek. Making his way across the refuse-choked stream, Gordon came to an open patch where a group of headless bodies, each with its severed head posed on the right shoulder, lay in pools of blood.

This, Gordon often said, was one of the worst moments of his life. His brain clouded with anger. Going across to the dead Lar Wang, he picked up the head, wrapped it in a cloth, and set off for Li's HQ with the intention of confronting the Governor with this grisly proof of his treachery. Li, he raged, must be obliged to resign on the spot and taken back to Pekin in chains to await trial. If he made any attempt to resist, Gordon admitted later, he meant to hand back Soochow to the Tien Wang.

Fortunately for both men, Li had decided that once Gordon had discovered the truth, he would be a man to be avoided at all costs, and had ridden off to make his triumphal entry into the city. Even so Gordon obliged the guards to let him board the steamer, and there wrote out his demands and accusations in a lengthy document; then still clutching Lar Wang's head, he continued down river to Quinsan.

Li found the document on his return, but since it was written in English, a language he was unable to read, gave it to his liaison officer, Halliday Macartney, a level-headed Scot, for translation.

Realising what a scandal such a letter could create, Macartney contented himself with telling Li that Gordon was 'most upset' by what he had seen and that 'the letter had been written in a fit of indignation'.

Much as he must have resented such behaviour on the part of a 'foreigner', Li was only too well aware of the fact that, entirely due to Gordon's genius, the Ever Victorious Army was probably the corps d'élite of the imperial army, and its loss or degeneration might well be marked by a revival of the Tien Wang's fortunes on the battlefield. He made excuses. Repeating Ching's previous accusations, he assured Gordon in a letter which he confided to Macartney, that not only had the Wangs put up impossible counterdemands, but had tried to stir up the locals against the occupiers; their killing had in fact been ordered as a 'defensive measure'.

In Quinsan, a furious Gordon declared that he was not satisfied by Li's excuses and explanations. His threats redoubled. It was not enough, he told Macartney, that Li should be forced to resign; he must be publicly executed. Macartney was a very worried man. He saw plainly that this quarrel jeopardized European interests in the country. Frantic signals were sent to General Brown — who had taken over from General Staveley — and to Sir Frederick Bruce, now one of Gordon's greatest admirers, to urge a more reasonable and more diplomatic outlook. But Gordon was in one of his most difficult moods. Even a personal attempt on the part of the Emperor himself at appeasement, in the shape of a decoration and 10,000 taels in cash, accompanied by a letter of thanks for his great services, only called forth the frigid reply that 'after what had occurred at Soochow, he (Gordon) was unable to accept any mark of His Majesty's favour, and therefore begs His Majesty to receive his thanks for his intended kindness, and allow him to decline the same'.

It was the first time in history that an individual had dared to refuse a gift from the Imperial Throne. But for the fact that the Emperor was a clear sighted man who, like Li, saw clearly the value of Gordon's continued presence at the head of the Ever Victorious Army, Gordon might well have considered himself lucky to get away with mere dismissal.

Finally it was once again his pride in his beloved 'army' which brought him back into the field after a semi-reconciliation with Li. With Gordon sulking in his tent, his men were enjoying the inactivity of garrison life, and spending large cash bonuses which Li was issuing to provoke those very moral lapses which he guessed shrewdly would stir Gordon into some positive reaction. He was not mistaken. There was still a lot more fighting to be done, and Gordon was determined that no battle should be fought without the Ever Victorious Army. He agreed at last to a meeting.

The result was a typical oriental compromise. Gordon accepted to place himself *nominally* under Li's command, provided that the latter would acknowledge publicly that the Wangs had been executed on his personal order. Li agreed to do this, but no mention of a specific date for the publication of the 'confession' was made, thus offering a convenient 'face-saving' loophole, while at the same time Gordon was able to salve his conscience by asserting in a letter to Sir Frederick Bruce 'Had I left the imperialists to fend for themselves, hostilities might last another six years, whereas I do not apprehend the rebellion will last six months longer if I take the field.'

Bruce was an able man, ambitious for his country, and unusually far sighted. The silk trade was a rich plum for the British foreign market, but the principal silk producing area was situated between Soochow and Nanking, scene of constant fighting. Prosperity could only be restored by the Taipings' final defeat, and the imperial victory, he was convinced, depended on Gordon continuing in command. It was also a cherished hope that, the Taipings crushed, he would be able to arrange for Gordon to be posted to Pekin in the double role of Military Attaché and Minister of War to the Imperial Government. Yet he had to keep an eye on home opinion. Many people in England, especially in Whig (or Liberal) circles, still disapproved strongly of Britain's support of a 'heathen despot' against a 'Christian revolutionary movement designed to free the people of China from the bonds of tyranny.'

Gordon himself was deeply affected by the criticism levelled at him as 'the instrument of heathen repression' by the Shanghai consuls who went as far as to 'beg' him not to give Li any further help. Grimly he ignored them. It was his duty — more, it was God's will — that he crush the rebels. And this being the case, no earthly power could dissuade him from being the instrument of His will. Nevertheless it was a great solace to receive a letter from Sir Frederick Bruce after the relief of Kiangsu, ending — 'in relieving it (the Kiangsu province) from being the battlefield of the insurrection and in restoring it to its suffering inhabitants . . . you may assure yourself that you are rendering a true service to humanity as well as to great national interests. . .'

Late February (1864), the Ever Victorious Army moved out of Quinsan into the region between Soochow and Nanking.

In the early days of this new campaign it looked as though Gordon's fabled luck and the Ever Victorious Army's capacity to triumph on the battlefield, were past history. After a few minor successes, an attack on the town of Kintang was a complete failure. Gordon was hit in the leg and carried on till he fainted from loss of blood, but his collapse was the signal for a general retreat.

The fact that his aura of invulnerability had been dissipated became world headlines. The Taipings announced they would soon be marching on Shanghai and Pekin. There was consternation in imperial circles, while the British Prime Minister, Lord Palmerston, stated in the House of Commons 'Major Gordon, I am sorry to see by the last accounts, has sustained a check and been wounded . . . I hope not severely. He is a most able and distinguished officer. . .'

Rebel jubilation gave signs of being justified. Forced to rest while his leg healed, Gordon was unable to lead an attack on Waissoo on the last day of March, and once again the Ever Victorious Army was repulsed with heavy losses. In this same action General Ching was killed, his death, rather surprisingly in view of their bitter disputes in the past, causing Gordon the most acute distress.

But a week later, though limping, Gordon was back in command. From that moment Taiping triumphs were proved to have been a mere flash in the pan. As the Ever Victorious Army's morale rose after a number of successful actions, that of the Taipings fell, paving the way for Gordon's last — and in many ways most dramatic — victory in China; the storming of the great stronghold of Changchow, held by 20,000 Taipings commanded by Hu Wang, one of their ablest commanders, notorious for his squint and his cruelty.

The final assault was made on May 11. After a heavy bombardment, Gordon ordered the advance at one o'clock in the afternoon. Murderous fire held up the first column, which appeared to waver. 'At this critical moment', an eye witness wrote, 'Gordon gave the signal for his men to go forward. They raced up into the breach with Gordon at their head. Hart (inspector of customs at Shanghai) who was standing with Li on a nearby hill, saw the two attacks, saw the imperialists hesitate, saw Gordon's column rush forward through showers of missiles, saw Gordon himself standing out against the skyline, the first to mount the breach.

'Then for one terrible moment, the onlookers held their breath. Facing the breach at one hundred and fifty paces distant, stood the grim 32 pounder of the *Firefly,* its muzzle crammed with grape and pointing straight at the breach where Gordon stood. Was he to be blown to pieces in his very hour of triumph? The gunners took aim, but the gun was silent. The Taipings had neglected the Cromwellian precept and had not kept their powder dry! So Gordon at the head of his troops swept on into the town unscathed. . .'

Two months later, Hung, the Tien Wang, besieged in his capital of Nanking, his brain failing, hanged his wives then committed suicide by drinking a mixture of gold leaf and wine. A further nineteen days passed before the imperial force, some 80,000 strong, managed to blow an enormous breach in the 'Heavenly Capital's' ramparts, through which they stormed slaughtering everybody on sight. 'Of those not killed defending the city, 7,000 were put to death after capture; most of the rest took their own lives. . .'

It was the end of a rebellion which had lasted twelve years and at times came dangerously near to success. And, but for the presence of one man, a 'foreigner', the Manchu dynasty might well have been chased from the throne; a foreigner as fanatical in his quieter way as the self-styled Heavenly King and Younger Brother of Christ; a foreigner who from then on was to be known as 'Chinese Gordon.'

Especially in England!

Britain was then reaching the apogee of the imperial era. Heroes were popular. They were living proof of the superiority of the Island Race. Gordon was typical of an age in which, to quote one biographer, 'The British army could be relied upon to produce a junior officer capable of pacifying a frontier, quelling a rebellion, or administering an empire. . .'

The only award that Gordon would accept for his share in the Taiping downfall was the Order of the Yellow Jacket. It was the most cherished of all Chinese decorations, dating from the time of the Manchu invasion when the Emperor, afraid that he might be singled out for a determined attack by some dedicated enemy bent on his destruction, ordered every man of his personal bodyguard of forty warriors to wear a yellow jacket of exactly the same pattern as that which he himself wore, a garment till then considered as an emblem of royalty. In keeping with tradition, membership of the order was limited to forty. Contrary to the custom of the day, Gordon rejected all proposals of monetary awards, and afterwards liked to stress, perhaps somewhat smugly, that he left China poorer than the day he arrived.

His task accomplished, he was unable to make up his mind as to what he should do next. He hated the idea of returning to England, yet took it upon himself to disband the Ever Victorious Army, feeling that with no more fighting in prospect, this tough band of mercenaries might well form the nucleus of another revolutionary movement. He would have liked to have been taken on as Military Attaché to the Pekin court, or else as commander of the new force the Shanghai merchants were thinking of financing, but at the same time was influenced by a strong feeling of duty to his parents. He had promised to be 'back in England by Christmas '64', and in the end it was this sense of duty which prevailed.

A passage home was booked for mid-October.

It was while waiting to sail, and rather at a loose end, that he was overcome by an acute guilt complex. His successes, the honours the Chinese Court wished to shower on him, the way people in England spoke of his exploits, the flattering comments of the British Minister — 'Lieutenant Colonel Gordon well deserves Her Majesty's favour for, independently of the skill and courage he has shown, his disinterestedness has elevated our national character in the eyes of the Chinese. . .', instead of bringing him satisfaction, upset him profoundly. It was all the work of the Devil — he was a firm believer in the physical existence of Satan — designed to lure him into the deadly sin of pride, and while everyone was intent on rewarding him, all he wished was to be humiliated as a punishment for his vanity and self-satisfaction; in short, the Devil had set the trap, and he, Gordon, had tumbled into it. He was overcome by melancholy by the mere fact that he was alive when, as in the Crimea, he had longed for death on the battlefield.

Terrified that he would be given a public welcome in England, he wrote to his parents that the 'individual' could be expected home in December, adding that 'no attention whatsoever must mark the occasion of the "individual's" return.'

The day he was due to embark he managed to avoid any form of farewell party or reception. Slipping unnoticed on board his old HQ the *Hyson,* which was to take him downstream to the docks, he locked himself in his cabin, even going to the extent of having his new clothes wrapped in a bundle and trailed overboard to give them a shabby, worn appearance before putting them on for the first time. However, he was not altogether successful in his attempt to get away incognito. According to one source — 'the mess humoured him: not so the local Chinese. They all knew that their General Gordon was leaving them, and the *Hyson* found herself sailing between banks beflagged, lit by hundreds of lanterns and lined by troops, while crackers, guns, gongs and horns, sped the deliverer on his way. . .'

3

The Limbo

Although perfectly genuine when stressing the wish that his return to England should pass unheralded, Gordon may have been a little surprised that he was not obliged to make any effort to avoid being lionised. The truth was that fame is often short-lived, and in the months that had passed since the fall of Soochow, other events had ousted 'Chinese Gordon' from the limelight.

On disembarkation, he went straight to his parents' home, shared by the austere Augusta, at 5 Rockstone Place, Southampton, where he found life unchanged since his boyhood, and where 'Chinese Gordon' was simply a member of the family who had spent some years abroad and who was expected to conform rigidly with unwritten household laws, such as attending morning prayers and restricting his compulsive smoking to the kitchen and then only after the cook had gone to bed.

He was quite content to fall into this uninspired routine, even, as one contemporary remarked, acting 'ADC to his mother, going out with her in the carriage and assisting with the shopping'. As for honours, he unbent grudgingly to accept a C.B., but was adamant in his refusal to attend any official function, carrying his self-effacement to the extent of refusing to discuss his experiences in China. On one occasion when he found that his mother was planning to have his diaries published, he flew into a violent rage, demanded their immediate return then hurled them into the fire. It was a stupid action. The diaries would have proved of the greatest value to future historians.

In view of the fact that he had shown such talent for handling non-British troops, it was surprising that at the end of his leave he was not posted either to Africa or India, but his successes in China had aroused mixed feelings at the War Office. A number of his contemporaries were undoubtedly jealous. It was also suggested that he was 'a little unorthodox in his tactics and administration, a man who might too easily "go native", or forget that his duty was to uphold British interests, not to reform foreign governments'. As a result, his next posting could hardly have been more prosaic, nor in greater contrast with the command of the Ever Victorious Army. He was appointed Commander of Royal Engineers, Gravesend, his specific task the supervision of the building of five new forts to 'deny enemy access to the Thames Estuary'. It was not surprising that he considered that he was being deliberately pushed into a backwater.

A man of lesser character might have regarded the job as a sinecure and lapsed into a state of apathy. This was not Gordon's way. He got down to the task in hand with the same purposeful vigour and energy that he had shown in the direction of the siege of Quinsan.

After a few days at Gravesend, he wrote a long report to the War Office saying that the forts had been so badly sited that their construction was a waste of time and money. And even when the War Office, outraged, replied that he was entirely mistaken, ordering him to proceed with the work forthwith, he accepted the rebuff and set about completing the project in record time.

His presence electrified the garrison.

Till then a posting to Gravesend was looked upon as a rest cure by all ranks. Gordon lost no time in dispelling the illusion. 'To the dismay of his men' it was reported 'he arrived on the dot of eight every morning, after having urged his watermen to row him to his headquarters at twice the normal speed. He would leap ashore and almost run from place to place while junior officers, foremen, and contractors puffed after him! All ranks of the garrison found him an equally exacting taskmaster! This went on till two o'clock in the afternoon. He would not tolerate a mid-morning break.'

Unfortunately for Gordon's sense of restless energy, regulations laid down six hours per day as the time limit for parades. This meant that as he insisted on these six hours being worked at a single stretch, when two o'clock in the afternoon struck, living alone as he did and being a highly uncompanionable individual, for the rest of the day he was left a prey to what he called 'the doles'. This was all the more redoubtable as he had no hobbies and no love of the arts. Music left him cold. Most literature he dismissed as 'sinful'; yet another of the Devil's many manifestations.

During his off duty hours he fell victim to religious melancholia, enforcing on himself a semi-monastic regime, his only permitted relaxation lengthy Bible-reading sessions, and the writing of abstruse tracts to the humourless Augusta, the principal theme invariably 'how to subdue the body and uplift the spirit'. In this mood 'he prayed to be delivered from envy and ambition, for strength to resist the cigars and cigarettes he enjoyed in vast numbers, the brandy and sherry that gave an illusion of peace. He proved again and again, beyond any shadow of doubt, that the body was utterly evil. . .'

With winter approaching and with nothing to do other than brood on his imagined wickedness and shortcomings, he

took to going out at night, his pockets filled with tracts which
he scattered haphazard as he walked. Sometimes when he was
obliged to travel by train, he would throw bundles of them
out of the carriage window as he passed through built up
areas. His death wish became a mania translating itself in an
extraordinary Christmas message to Augusta — 'I will not say
many of them (happy Christmases) for our joy is in the Lord,
and we cannot wish many years will pass before He comes to
deliver us from our contemptible bodies. . .'

At this stage, with his guilt complex needled by inactivity
and — what he himself did not realise — sheer boredom, he
gives the impression of hovering on the brink of insanity. As
this brooding melancholia was aggravated by a self-imposed
near starvation regime, it is a tribute to his remarkable
physique that he survived this phase without doing lasting
damage to his health. His diet consisted almost entirely of
bread and tea, the two sometimes mixed together to form a
revolting mess, occasionally helped out by a little salt beef. It
was very fortunate that eventually he found an outlet for his
emotions. Quite suddenly he decided to devote all his off
duty hours to helping the poor, much in evidence in
Gravesend.

In this activity, he was helped by a Quaker couple, Mr
and Mrs Freese, who ran the local branch of the Religious
Tract Society. When, much to their surprise, the Freeses learnt
that 'the Colonel' was interested in their work, they sent him
an invitation to tea. It was possibly the only invitation he
ever accepted willingly.

The Freeses, a rather unsophisticated couple, had no idea
that their guest was none other than 'Chinese Gordon', but in
spite of one or two tactless remarks due to ignorance, about
China and the Christian Taipings, Gordon recognised their
essential goodness, with the result that this incongruous trio
became firm friends.

As C.R.E., Gordon occupied the Fort House, an
enormous building with a vast garden. He would have

preferred humbler quarters, and before his meeting with the Freeses had turned the garden over to be parcelled off into allotments so that the needy could grow their own fruit and vegetables. Then, helped by his new friends, he converted Fort House into a youth club. Except for a small apartment he kept for himself, every room was made into a meeting place, class room, or dormitory. He called the boarders his 'scuttlers'. They were entirely dependent on his charity. The money to feed and clothe them came from his own pocket. In his later days at Gravesend, he was buying 'suits by the score and boots by the gross'. He was not only benefactor but teacher, giving instruction in reading, writing, elementary mathematics, and insisting on detailed study of the Bible.

Towards the end he found he was running short of funds. This did not discourage him. Instead of cutting down on expenses, he began to sell everything he could lay hands on. As one friend said 'Nothing could quench his ardour. Neither shortage of money nor, as sometimes happened, failure to reform the habits and thinking of one of the less virtuous 'scuttlers' could turn him away from his mission. It was not so much that he was conquering boredom. Far more important, he had found an outlet for his missionary zeal and an escape from the loneliness of being a misfit in human society. . .'

Yet even during these moments of happiness — probably the only time in his life he was genuinely happy — he still looked forward to death, making a great point of visiting the dying and telling them how lucky they were. One Christmas, he spent his entire leave nursing one of his 'scuttlers' dying of typhoid, hoping that he too would contract the disease. Once his boat sank close to the bank. His reaction was expressed in a letter to Mrs. Freese, regretting that the accident had not occurred in midstream — 'if it had been in the middle I should be at home tonight in a very bright and happy land, for Death is the glorious gate to eternity, to glory and joy, unmixed with a taint of sorrow. . .'

This Gordonian utopia came to an end in 1871 when he was offered the post of British representative on the Danube Commission sitting at Galatz, on the Rumanian Black Sea coast.

Prior to this he had been struck by a renewed yearning to get out of the British Isles when he learnt that Sir Charles Napier was to lead an expedition to Abyssinia. He had asked to be attached to the expedition, but Sir Charles had turned down the request. Gordon was furious, indulged in a fit of sulks, and for several days refused to see anyone; even the Freeses.

In September, however, came the posting to Galatz, and the departure from Gravesend. He left quietly after giving all his furniture to the Freeses and his Chinese treasures to Augusta.

The new job was very well paid by the standards of the day — £2,000 a year — and could have proved interesting.

Rumania acted as a buffer state between decadent Turkey and aggressive Russia.

For over three hundred years known as the Danubian principalities of Moldavia and Wallachia, Rumania had been part of the Turkish dominions, or, as it was better known, the Ottoman Empire. Overrun in the early days of the Crimean war by the Russian army, it had been made a protectorate by the Treaty of Paris while remaining nominally under Turkish sovereignty. By 1871, locally administered by a constitutional figurehead, Prince Charles of Hohenzollern, and enjoying a considerable measure of autonomy, the country was moving towards full independence. Already politicians foresaw that the 'Rumanian problem' might well spark off the next Turco-Russian war, looked upon as inevitable. The purpose of the Commission was, therefore, to ensure freedom of navigation of the Danube.

For anyone with a taste for the subterfuges of espionage and behind-the-scenes diplomacy, Galatz would have been a choice posting. But the life of the Commission members involved them in those very activities which Gordon so genuinely detested; dinners, receptions, dances. It is difficult to understand why he accepted the position in the first place without protest. Once arrived he seemed determined to hate Galatz, Rumania, the Rumanians, and each individual member of the Commission, a dislike his fellow members soon reciprocated most heartily.

The appointment lasted a bare twelve months. On the way back to England, dispirited and with no idea what the future might hold for him, Gordon halted his journey to visit Constantinople. By pure chance the day that he made an official call on the British Ambassador, the Egyptian Prime Minister, Nubar Pasha, was also at the Embassy to pay his respects, the reason for his visit being to find a British officer to succeed Sir Samuel Baker, the famous explorer, as Governor of the Sudanese province of Equatoria.

Though Egypt was officially a Turkish possession, control from Constantinople was largely nominal, and Mohammed Ali, grandfather of Ismail the reigning Khedive (Viceroy) had been anxious to employ British officers to help run the country.

Nubar knew all about 'Chinese Gordon'. When they met he was not in the least rebuffed by Gordon's austere, unfriendly manner, and for his part, Gordon took a liking to the polished Egyptian. On Nubar's pressing invitation he postponed his departure for England for the time to pay a flying visit to Cairo. There, despite his repugnance for the 'dirtiness' of Cairo, he immediately accepted the Khedive's offer to become Equatoria's new Governor, provided the War Office agreed.

The fact that the province, from all he could gather, was in a state of chaos only served to fire his enthusiasm, especially as the Khedive made it clear that his principal task would be the suppression of the slave trade; furthermore, short as was his stay in the Egyptian capital, it was long enough for him to fall under the spell of the Khedive's renowned personal charm.

Ismail was an excellent judge of humanity and aware of his own power. Over the next few years he was one of the few able to reason with Gordon when the latter was in one of his black moods. Yet, as a result of one of those strange, unreasonable, changes of heart, becoming more and more frequent as he grew older, Gordon took a sudden and violent dislike to Nubar, to whom he referred as a 'low born Armenian whom he distrusted profoundly'.

It was only when he was back in England and had received War Office approval, and had had time to give the matter a little calm consideration, that the magnitude of the task he had accepted became clear.

By 1874, the slave trade had reached terrifying proportions. The first cargo of miserable black slaves, often referred to as 'black ivory' had been ferried across the Atlantic by the first Elizabeth's admiral Hawkins as far back as 1590. Since that date it was reckoned that some fifty million Africans, men, women, and children, had been dragged from their villages, marched in chain gangs to the coast, and there crowded into the infamous 'slavers' for the long crossing under such criminal conditions that many failed to survive.

Although officially slavery had been abolished, it still thrived in Arab countries, and above all in Egypt. The attitude of the Moslem world was directly opposed to that of the Christian on this question. The Prophet Mohammed himself had given his blessing to the principle of household slaves, though stipulating that they should be treated as members — albeit lowly ones — of the household. The fact remained, however, that whatever the degree, they were still slaves, and this the European powers was not prepared to tolerate.

It is probable that the Khedive's zeal, so loudly

proclaimed, in abolishing slavery throughout his dominions was prompted more by state and personal interests, than moral principles. He himself was heavily in debt; Egypt on the verge of bankruptcy.

National debts were first incurred by Ismail's uncle, Said Pasha, over the building of the recently completed Suez Canal. Instead of producing hard cash for his share in the construction, as was the case with France, Germany, Austria and Britain, Said had promised to supply the labour force. As he was unable to fulfil his promise, he found himself facing compensation claims from the other powers. The matter was put to arbitration, Napoleon III being appointed judge. The Emperor's verdict went against the unfortunate Khedive, who was left with no alternative other than to borrow. A sum of over three million pounds was advanced by Messrs Fruhling and Goschen at such a high rate of interest that there was little chance of it ever being reduced, let alone refunded.

Inheritor of these debts, incapable of cutting down his personal spending, Ismail could still see that near bankruptcy was a threat not only to his position as Khedive, but to Egyptian independence. He realised how expanding European influence had often been based on the take-over of a bankrupt state with the excuse of 'protecting national interests'. At the same time many of the slavers were growing too powerful. One in particular, Zubehr, even called himself the 'Black Khedive'. 'He affected royal state, kept a pair of lions on leash, and melted down twenty five thousand silver dollars to make bullets against his enemies protected by magic'. He had also raised his own army, a small but well trained band of mercenaries, superior on the battlefield to the underpaid, ill-equipped, low-spirited Egyptian units.

Weighing matters up, Ismail decided that if he were to issue a decree to the effect that slavery was to be abolished in his domains, he would be able to count on the wholehearted support of Europe and especially of Britain. If he could then extend his rule not only *de jure* but *de facto* to the Sudan by eliminating such men as Zubehr, he would be able to levy taxes which Zubehr and his like were putting in their own pockets, and perhaps, if he were careful, indulge for his own profit in the 'black ivory trade' on a reduced scale. It would be even better if an Englishman were appointed to direct this operation by which he hoped to persuade Europe that 'wherever the Egyptian flag flew, no matter how far flung, life and liberty were the sacred rights of all. . .'. There was another advantage. Should operations against the slavers fail, failure could be laid on the shoulders of the British officer in charge.

In spite of communiqués announcing successes, Sir Samuel Baker, Equatoria's first English governor, had achieved very little. As a cynic observed, 'he was a fine explorer but no organizer, and certainly no military genius'. During his tenure of office some of the slavers suspended their activities temporarily, or else went about them with greater circumspection, but there was no question of the trade being stamped out. Ismail eventually concluded that Sir Samuel was not the man for the job, and sent Nubar Pasha to Constantinople to find out whether the British Ambassador had any suggestions for a replacement. He was delighted by Nubar's choice, and certain, from the moment they met that, tactfully handled, Gordon was the answer to his prayers.

As soon as he arrived in Cairo, Gordon made a gesture which many claim to have been a grave psychological error.

Baker's salary had been fixed at £10,000 a year. Gordon demanded that this be slashed to £2,000. By so doing he hoped to impress on the Khedive and the world in general that he was a man entirely devoted to duty. He must show his new master 'gold and silver are not worshipped by all the world. They are powerful gods, but not as powerful as our God!'

Ismail was indeed impressed, but not in the way Gordon had hoped. Being himself so materially minded, he could not believe that any man could throw away £8,000 a year unless he were playing some subtle game. His suspicions aroused, he appointed an American of French descent, Colonel Chaillé-Long, as his personal liaison officer with Equatoria's new governor, but gave Gordon a free hand in choosing the rest of his staff. This Gordon proceeded to do, selecting three Englishmen, three Germans, a second American, an Italian, a Frenchman, and an Egyptian. In this heterogenous choice he revealed another fundamental weakness; his poor judgment of character and the capabilities of others.

This fault was shown up especially in his choice of the Egyptian, Abu Saud, picked because of his love of flying in the face of convention. Abu Saud had himself been a slaver, and was actually in gaol waiting trial for murder. From the practical point of view, Gordon's excuse could have been that he was observing the theory of 'set a thief to catch a thief', but in fact he was flattering himself that he was obeying the Divine principle of giving a sinner his chance of redemption.

This ill-assorted group proved useless as a unit. The only one to show any talent, stamina, or basic loyalty, was the Italian, Romolo Gessi. This was most unfortunate for Gordon, for the task set him was colossal. At the last moment the Khedive had told him that not only was he expected to put an end to the slave trade, but to extend Egyptian rule as far south as Uganda and the Great Lakes.

Even the journey to Equatoria was in itself a major undertaking.

From Cairo he took the train to Suez, where he embarked for the Red Sea port of Suakin. From Suakin it was a 240 mile camel ride to Berber on the Nile. From Berber to Khartoum, capital of the Sudan, was an easy stretch on the comparative comfort of a river steamer. But from Khartoum to his own capital of Gondokoro was the best part of a thousand miles, much of which would have to be covered on foot.

Whether due to natural impatience or a desire to impress

his entourage with his own physical fitness is not clear, but Gordon tackled this two thousand mile journey as if he were competing in an Olympic marathon, or as if his very life depended on its completion in the shortest possible time.

The record for the Suakin-Berber road stood at twelve days. Yet although Gordon was riding a camel for the first time in his life, he reduced this time by three days, exhausting his escort and nearly killing the camels. It was the same story once they were embarked on the steamer for Khartoum. 'He (Gordon) kept exhorting the stokers to get up more steam until they were blowing as hard as their own boilers. And when the steamer ran aground, he took off his trousers and leaped into the river to lend a personal hand.' In this way he achieved the fastest ever run between Berber and Khartoum and by producing a copy of the *Pall Mall Gazette,* dated February 13, since the day he stepped onto the quay at Khartoum was March 13, claimed that he had reduced the journey from London to Khartoum to exactly one month.

All these 'records' seemed to indicate an auspicious beginning for Equatoria's new governor, but almost immediately after setting foot in the Sudanese capital, he was quarrelling violently with the Egyptian Governor General of the Sudan, Ayoub Pasha, a French-educated Circassian. Ayoub, for his part, went out of his way to be friendly. As the steamer docked, he was on the quayside in full dress uniform. There was a battalion strength Guard of Honour; a military band playing 'God Save The Queen'. After the two men had greeted each other, Ayoub gave his subordinate — as Gordon was in his capacity of Governor of Equatoria — a pressing invitation to a banquet the following evening. With his horror of all social events, Gordon accepted with a bad grace.

The evening confirmed his worst fears. Ayoub Pasha, influenced by his Parisian upbringing, adored good living, and fondly imagined that all Europeans had similar tastes. Gordon arrived in a bad temper. Just before leaving his quarters he had found two of his servants drunk and given them a sound beating. Having done so, he was promptly plunged in gloom at his own lack of self-control.

From the start everything about the banquet exasperated him; there was too much to eat, too much to drink. He was impressed by a display of war dances by wild Dinka tribesmen, but when the warriors were replaced by a troupe of dancing girls, his puritanism was so outraged that, causing great offence to his host, he got up and stalked out.

Nor was he in the least ashamed of his tactlessness and bad manners. On the contrary, he flattered himself that he had taught Ayoub to respect 'British morality'. He went even further. When he returned the Governor General's hospitality, he gave him 'a lesson in simplicity' by feeding him tapioca pudding on chipped plates. And 'there were also lessons in how not "to cajole a member of the Gordon family" which were administered by the blunt method of telling the Governor-General and anyone else who tried to argue with him, to shut up and go away.'

After the shortest possible time in Khartoum, Gordon was off on the final stage of over a thousand miles to Gondokoro, through mostly desolate marsh land — the *sudd* — as unhealthy as the swamps of Bengal or Assam. On his steamer the *Bordein,* he complained that 'huge rats gambolled and fought in the cabin. . . harvest bugs, sand flies, mosquitoes swarmed, sucked, stung . . .' and commenting ruefully on the mosquitoes, he added 'the proboscis is formed like a bayonet with a hinge at the bend; they turn it down for perforation and press on it with their head muscles and chest. . .'

But the series of records was maintained. After unpleasant incidents with the crew whom he accused of laziness, and slapping the captain's face for siding with the crew, Gordon had the satisfaction of reaching Gondokoro in twenty-eight days, thus almost halving the normal time.

The new Governor was not impressed by the first contact with his capital. It was 'in the last degree squalid'. He compared it with 'a Wild West outpost'; an agglomeration of baked mud huts protected by a stockade. Being in the middle of essentially hostile territory, few of the inhabitants dared to wander beyond easy running distance of the gates. Of the five hundred strong garrison, Gordon said 'Never in the course of my life have I seen such wretched creatures dignified by the name of soldiers. As for the officers, they were as brave as hares. . .' He had soon reached the conclusion that though they were armed with rifles, tribes-men skilled in the use of spear and shield would have little difficulty in routing such an ill-trained, gutless rabble. To make matters worse, he soon found out that the commander, Raouff, was accepting bribes to turn a blind eye to the activities of local slavers, while the men spent all their pay — when they were lucky enough to get it — on slave girls and gin.

After sending Raouff packing, he wrote an angry report to London in which he blamed the deplorable state of affairs existing in Equatoria on Ayoub Pasha. The Governor General, he claimed, was immoral and corrupt. How could he expect his subordinates to be otherwise? His anger was also directed against Sir Samuel Baker for sending in what, he insisted, was a deliberately false picture of the progress of the war against the slavers.

This done, he made two important decisions. First he would return at once to Khartoum to confront Ayoub with his iniquities, and second, he would convey to the Khedive a demand — backed by the threat of resignation should the demand be ignored — that Equatoria be confided to him as a totally independent command.

The Governor-General was far from happy when the killjoy Gordon was back again in Khartoum a bare two months after his departure. He bowed patiently before the storm of Gordon's reproaches, and made no attempt to check the flow of telegrams to Cairo demanding the severing of all links between Gondokoro and Khartoum.

Ismail had probably foreseen such an eventuality and made no effort to uphold Ayoub's authority, even in theory. Convinced that in Gordon he held a trump card, every request was granted immediately. In future Gordon was to have a free hand in the running of Equatoria.

Delighted by such an easy victory, Gordon raced down to Berber where he picked up the rest of the staff. Then, barely giving them time to change steamers, was off at the same mad pace for Gondokoro.

4

A Lesson in Governorship

Back in Gondokoro, Gordon was again struck by the colossal responsibilities he would be called upon to shoulder.

The territory was vast; the size of the whole of western Europe including Scandinavia. Communications, other than the river, were non-existent. The population was divided into two ethnic groups; Arab and Moslem, Negro and animist. The dominant Arabs were mostly descendants of Mohammed Ali's conquering armies and had enriched themselves by the slave trade. Two thousand miles from Cairo, they had no intention of submitting to Khedival law. As for the negroes, as Gordon noted 'they had lived so long with this traffic in human beings, that though its victims, they had come to accept it as an inevitable part of their lives. A family (negro) would willingly exchange a child for a cow. . .'

Sir Samuel Baker had more or less given up struggling, but Gordon was a fighter who revelled in facing up to impossible odds. His first decrees emphasized that trading in slaves could entail the most severe punishment; possibly death. Further laws proclaimed that private trade in ivory (white) was forbidden, as from then on ivory would be a government monopoly, and forbade the import of arms and ammunition.

Gordon was under no illusions as to the efficacy of mere decrees. Experience in China had taught him that, certainly to begin with, respect for laws had to be won by successful action against law-breakers, and in itself posed a serious problem. The troops at his disposal, as has been seen, were of the poorest quality. His staff was little better. The mediocrity of most members of his staff was not helped by his ever increasing dislike of delegating responsibility. This mistrust of others proved a grave handicap. It meant, amongst other things, that he could never inspire a second-rate officer to rise above himself — one of the secrets of a truly great leader — while those who were efficient were continuously irritated by his obvious lack of confidence in their capabilities. On the other hand when it was a question of the 'rank and file', especially non-European, the picture was totally different. Few people have ever inspired the ordinary soldier as he did. In the heat of battle, his quite exceptional bravery had the power to weld a rabble into a victory-winning force.

From a nucleus of forty mercenaries who had been his predecessor's bodyguard, and whom he nicknamed 'Baker's forty thieves', he set to work to train the wretched Egyptian soldiers comprising the garrison — in his desperate search for fighting material, he even recruited a group of black cannibals — and at the earliest opportunity led them himself on a punitive expedition against the slavers.

He had accomplished a near miracle. In the very first encounter a caravan of three hundred slaves and two hundred head of stolen cattle was captured, a miniature victory followed up by several equally successful brushes with local Arab chiefs. In these brief, but often ferocious actions, Gordon's luck held. In the wilds of Africa, as in China, he seemed to be immune from bullet and spear.

Though it could not be claimed that these reverses had broken the slavers, their losses made them realise that, for the time being at any rate, they would have to curb their activities. Above all it was brought home to them that the new Governor was a power to be reckoned with. When in late summer they learnt that, under the influence of a judicious mixture of bribes and threats, Gordon had persuaded some of their fellow traders to change sides, that hundreds of slaves had been waylaid in transit and liberated, a general decision was taken to play a waiting game and put up an outward show of acquiescence to the irksome laws issued by the tiresome Governor.

Curbing slaver activities was, however, only a part of Gordon's task. When it came to physical action he could always be relied on to gain the upper hand. Fighting to raise the morale and standard of living of the browbeaten, cowed, negro population was another matter. A born fighter himself, their spineless acceptance of misfortune shocked and infuriated him. With his usual missionary zeal, he tried to instil some standards of 'civilization', as he termed it, into their daily lives; one such standard being an appreciation of currency.

Till his arrival, such commerce as there was had been conducted on a basis of barter. 'I began by paying each man who worked' he wrote, describing his efforts to make the negroes money-minded, 'some beads. Next day I gave each man who worked half a piastre in copper and offered to sell him beads to that amount. Today I made a first rate affair. A chief brought a tusk and wanted two bells for his cows to wear round their necks in exchange. I said "No. I will give you two dollars for the tusk." He said "Yes." So I gave him the two dollars. "Now" I said. "I will sell you two bells for a dollar each." '

Everyday Gordon was making his presence increasingly felt. Yet he could not be in every place where he was needed at the same time. As a result much of the good he achieved was nullified by his staff's inefficiency, or dishonesty; or both.

This became particularly manifest in the case of Abu Saud, the man whom, against all advice, Gordon had insisted on taking out of gaol. To begin with Gordon kept on saying in his letters home, that Abu Saud was the only member of his staff with 'any kick in him', going as far as to appoint him deputy Governor in Gondokoro while he himself was out in the bush on his slaver-hunting expeditions.

During his absence, Gordon was kept happy by a stream of reports from his deputy that the heads of surrounding tribes were, one after the other, making their submission to the central authority, and only too anxious to be good and loyal subjects to the Khedive in the future.

He was so lulled by wishful thinking that it was some time before he discovered that Abu Saud was busy lining his pockets by trading on the side in ivory, thus contravening one of the principal laws he was supposed to enforce.

This first revelation of blatant treachery was a sad blow, and rather typical was Gordon's reaction to be seized by a loathing of the whole Egyptian race, especially when, to save his own skin, Abu Saud tried, unsuccessfully, to stir up a mutiny. It is difficult to understand why Gordon did not throw him into the local gaol. It is possible that he may have felt that such blatant evidence of disunity would have had a disturbing effect on those he was trying, so painstakingly, to govern. Saud was sent back to Egypt in disgrace, and Gordon, thoroughly disillusioned, vented his bad temper on all around him.

'A perfect tyrant, I am', he wrote to Augusta, 'But you want to be a tyrant among these people. They take advantage of your kindness' and he added on the subject of the Egyptian soldiers 'I look on the Chinese as far superior to them in every way. . .One's work is really more to reform the

Egyptians than to civilize the natives. . .'

Sickness had played havoc with his staff. Gondokoro was living up to its reputation as a 'white man's grave'. There was malaria and blackwater fever. Mosquitoes made life unbearable. Two of the Englishmen died. All the other Europeans, with the exception of Gordon, fell seriously ill. In the end Gordon found that he was running his little empire single handed, at the same time obliged to act as doctor and nurse to his stricken officers. It is probable that but for his sudden decision to abandon Gondokoro to the triumphant mosquito, and move his Headquarters to higher ground, not one would have survived.

At the new capital, Lado, on a bluff overlooking the river, the sick men began to convalesce, only to be faced with trouble of a different kind. Physically exhausted, nerves frayed, Gordon quarrelled with everyone on the slightest excuse, the only moments of peace enjoyed by his staff being when he would shut himself up in his tent for hours on end with his Bible and a bottle of brandy.

In October, the French-American Chaillé-Long returned from a mission to the self-styled King of the Buganda (later Uganda) territory, Mutesa, to persuade this monarch that it would be to his advantage to acknowledge the Khedive as his sovereign, and continue as a reigning vassal under Cairo's distant and nebulous protection.

Mutesa was one of the few black African chiefs who had been able to defy the Arab slavers, and Chaillé-Long was able to extract a verbal agreement from his host. It had proved to be rather a frightening experience. The Bugandans had never seen a horse. When Chaillé-Long dismounted, they thought he was some kind of centaur who somehow or other had come to pieces. He was rather amused by the consternation he had caused, but his amusement was short lived once he had been shown into Mutesa's presence. 'At a nod from the King thirty subjects, chosen at random, had their heads bashed in. Mutesa politely explained that rough methods were the only ones effective for such a people as his!' Long then produced his presents, a mirror five foot by three, a music box which played *Il Trovatore,* and an electrical machine which 'he so regulated that while others were writhing on the ground unable to let go of the innocent looking terminals, he himself remained uninfluenced. The king was delighted. . .'

Gordon was pleased by this success. Relations between him and the Khedive's 'commissar' improved, but as one writer put it 'within a few weeks the brief honeymoon was over'. Soon Gordon was complaining to Augusta that 'he (Long) has tumbled back into procrastination and forgetfulness'. The only person of his entourage with whom Gordon was able to keep on reasonably good terms was the Italian, Romolo Gessi.

Unable to escape from his black moods, he now began to convince himself that his task was quasi-impossible, and, worse still, if he did succeed such a success would be contrary to the good of the population. His doubts were brought on by an ever growing dislike of the Arabo-Egyptian ruling classes. It was true that the locals had learnt to trust him, Gordon, as an individual. But his tour of governorship could not last for ever, and it was obvious that he would be replaced by some 'corrupt Egyptian'. 'What right have I' he asked 'to coax the natives to be quiet for them to fall into the hands of a rapacious Pasha after my departure. . .?'

He began to ponder the possibility of resignation, and came to the conclusion that he would ask the Khedive to relieve him of his duties once he had extended Equatoria's boundaries to the Great Lakes — Victoria, Nyanza and Albert. It was only the challenge presented by such an undertaking that preserved his mental balance, further undermined by increasing doubts as to whether what he was doing were justified from the moral point of view. He was heard to say — 'Man is a very fine animal when in the natural state. The grace with which these natives walk and run is remarkable. . .I should say they are singularly free of vice!' He was in fact beginning to agree with the explorer Livingstone that 'the native untouched by civilization is an honest, happy, if idle character, requiring no police or apparent code of law to keep his community in harmony. . .'

The need for action as the moment approached to set out for the lakes temporarily dispersed Gordon's depression. Technical and physical difficulties were immense, the former aggravated by his chronic mistrust of his staff. As one of them, a Lieutenant Chippendall, complained 'He seems to think no one but his blessed self can even scew a box lid on. He is a fearful egoist. If you give an opinion you are nailed at once, your reasons asked and worried at till out of sheer fag you agree to any proposition he likes to put forward. . .'

After several changes of plan, Gordon decided to travel as far as possible by river. Chippendall was sent off to establish river stations between Lado and Dufile, a distance of some 150 miles. From Dufile, acting on his own initiative, Chippendall pushed on up stream and on his return was able to inform Gordon that the river was definitely navigable as far as Lake Albert.

The start was delayed by the non-arrival of two river steamers, the *Khedive* and the *Nyanza,* held up south of Khartoum by freak floods. After waiting all May and most of June, Gordon had decided to risk the journey in native built boats (nuggars), and was on the point of setting out when, on July 12, the *Khedive* arrived. Gordon, however, was by then so angry that he opted to travel the hard way, in the nuggars.

It would have been wiser to have husbanded his strength, for his health was by then severely undermined by the enervating climate and tough daily life. Often the nuggars had to be hauled against the current and if one of them broke loose, as frequently happened, it would be swept miles downstream before being recovered. Even Gordon, glutton as he was for hardship, was discouraged. 'Often and often the ropes break' he noted in his diary 'and it all has to be done over again. I do not feel as if I can ever do any more work after this command.' He was also beginning to doubt whether Chippendall's report as to the river's navigability were correct. Four major difficulties faced him, he complained — '1st, the natural difficulties of the river, 2nd, the march through shy and unknown tribes who have never before seen a foreigner, 3rd, a useless and unreliable set of soldiers encumbered with women and children, 4th, want of good ropes to haul the nuggars . . . Anxiety has killed any enthusiasm in me. I never had a more anxious time.'

His troubles increased two days after writing these notes when, after losing two nuggars in the flood waters, he decided to camp near the village of Moogie. There, the tribes were not only 'shy and unknown'; they were actively hostile. Desultory attacks, easily repulsed, were made on the camp during the night, though next day, much to their annoyance, Gordon would not allow his men to retaliate by raiding the villages. But when the attacks were repeated the following night, he so far departed from his pro-black African attitude, that he ordered one of his officers, a young Frenchman Linant de Bellefonde, to take a detachment, find the nearest village and burn it.

This would-be punitive expedition ended in disaster. The patrol walked straight into an ambush, every man, including de Bellefonde, being slaughtered.

Gordon was in despair when he heard of the tragedy. He blamed himself for de Bellefonde's death. He should have known better than to have allowed an inexperienced young officer to set off in charge of such useless men. His dislike of Egyptian soldiers increased and he went as far as calling them 'cowardly, lying, effeminate brutes, without any good point about them.' 'I wish they had one neck' he added 'and someone would squeeze it. . .'

To his great relief the *Khedive* arrived at Moogie on September 13, but the very next day was caught in an eddy and swept on to the rocks. Continued efforts by every available man failed to move her. Gordon then sent a urgent message to Romolo Gessi asking him to come as quickly as possible with a properly equipped team, and made one of his lightening decisions. Rather than stay idle waiting for Gessi to arrive, he would try to push on overland, no matter what the risks and hardships involved. He had reached the village of Labore, when a messenger caught up with him with the news that the *Khedive* had been refloated.

He could have turned back, but unwisely decided to carry on on foot. The trek lasted twenty-seven days; an unrelieved nightmare. The rainy season was at its height. Not one of the tents was waterproof. Flies and leeches plagued him. 'I am nearly dead,' he wrote 'I never had such fatigue.' But after reaching Dufile, and temporarily leaving the jungle behind, his spirits began to revive; without justification.

On October 17, he recorded 'IT IS ALL OVER,' and he went on to explain, 'After marching a bare five miles, I fancied for some time I heard a voice like thunder which increased as we approached the river. At last we stood above it on a rocky bank covered with vegetation; and there it was, appalling to look at, far less to think of getting anything up or down, except in splinters, as it boiled down twisting into eddies . . . these shoots last for two miles . . . of course it is all over, the idea of taking up the screw steamer, the *nuggars*, or indeed anything. . .'

Gordon had in fact — though he found no joy in it — discovered the Fola Falls, a totally unnegotiable obstacle to any form of navigation. Only one course of action remained open. A message was sent back to Gessi, who by then had arrived at Lado, that the steamer *Nyanza* must be dismantled and brought overland in pieces on the backs of porters.

Much to his credit, Gessi succeeded in this seemingly impossible undertaking much to Gordon's delight. But by the time the *Nyanza* had been reassembled and was ready to make the first trip round Lake Albert — an event eagerly awaited not only by the Khedive, but also by the Royal Geographical Society — Gordon was in another of his moods.

He was afraid, he said, that if he were to be the 'God fated ravisher of the Virgin Lake' a gold medal might be conferred on him, and this was an eventuality he wished at all costs to avoid. Deliberately provocative one would say, since he admitted that both the Royal Geographical Society and the Khedive would be 'very much angered', he ordered Gessi to carry out this first exploration of Lake Albert, while he took it upon himself to march south, mapping the unknown territory to the Buganda border.

This proved to be an even longer and more exhausting trek; the country even more hostile, hot, damp, sticky, with insects both crawling and flying, whose stings were like 'jabs from a bayonet'. Nevertheless — and quite unnecessarily — Gordon insisted on maintaining a killing pace, as though deliberately trying to mortify his flesh, yet acutely miserable and aware of his physical suffering — 'The moment the sun goes down, a cold damp arises which enters one's very bones. There is not an interval of five minutes from the setting of the sun and the rising of the dreadful damp, and you feel the danger as it were at once. . .' He also recorded that he narrowly escaped being struck by lightning, was stung at least three times by scorpions, and that once a snake fell on his head from an overhanging branch.

By the time Mrooli, near the Buganda frontier, was reached, Gordon felt incapable of carrying on to meet the king, Mutesa, in person. Instead he sent his senior Sudanese officer Nuehr Agha, accompanied by an escort of 160 men, to carry his personal greetings to the black monarch and try to persuade him to agree to the establishment of an Egyptian garrison on his territory by the shores of Lake Victoria.

Once Nuehr Agha was on his way, Gordon made the journey down stream to Foweira by canoe, covering the seventy-two miles in thirty-six hours. He had hoped to carry straight on to Dufile, but a severe attack of malaria kept him in bed for several days. When at last he reached Dufile, he was able to record that he had been away six weeks during which time he had covered 400 miles in twenty days of marching through hitherto unexplored country.

A month later, back in his new capital, Lado, he found himself confronted with so many administrative problems, that again he was obliged to delegate to Gessi the task of ensuring that Lake Victoria was recognized as part of the Khedive's extended dominions. This comparatively sedentary stage was of brief duration. When Gessi returned, accompanied by another Italian explorer, Carlo Piaggia, he reported that he had sailed all round Lake Albert, and that the only river of any size flowing into it, which must be the Nile, came from Lake Victoria, thus disproving the explorer Richard Burton's theory that the Nile actually rose in Lake Tanganyika. Piaggia brought news of other rivers, just to add to the confusion, and though arrangements had been made for a spell of home leave, Gordon decided that this was a problem that he must settle to his own satisfaction before sailing for England.

Starting from Dufile, he made a long-delayed trip round Lake Albert on the *Nyanza,* during the course of which he received a message from Nuehr Agha, that Mutesa had agreed to the establishment of the proposed Egyptian garrison and to recognize Khedival authority, news which Gordon promptly forwarded to Cairo. From Lake Albert he pushed on by small boat to the Murchison Falls, and then, despite the fact that he was suffering from intermittent attacks of fever, set off on foot to explore, mapping as he went, seventy miles of dense jungle between Magungo and Foweira.

Nuehr Agha was waiting for him at Foweira with shattering news. The report of Mutesa's submission was false. In fact just the reverse was true. As a gesture of defiance, Mutesa had disarmed and imprisoned the 160 men of the escort, and turned Nuehr Agha loose to go back to warn his master that any infringement of Bugandan territory would be met with armed resistance.

Gordon was so disillusioned by his 'idle, deceitful and cowardly' soldiers that he gave up any idea of imposing his will by force. He was utterly discouraged, regretting his Chinese, their stolid courage and apparent indifference to suffering. But he still felt responsible for the fate of the prisoners, and since all thoughts of the strong arm policy had to be abandoned, the only alternative was diplomacy.

Luckily for Gordon, and also for the prisoners, he had engaged a German doctor, Edward Schnitzer, as his medical officer. Schnitzer had lived so long in Egypt and the Sudan, that he had become a Moslem and adopted the name of Emin. At that very moment, Emin, who was equally popular with both Arabs and black Africans, was in the neighbourhood. He was quite prepared to talk to Mutesa, conveying Gordon's promise — a promise which, in fact, he had no right to give — that in return for the release of the prisoners, Buganda's independence would be guaranteed. In just over a week, Emin was back with the 160 men who, after so many days of anguish believing that any moment they would be led out to be slaughtered, could scarcely believe that the nightmare was over.

There was one last reconnaissance to be carried out, and a visit to an isolated garrison installed eight months previously at Masindi, an important position in the Bunyoro country, also claimed by the Khedive, ruled by another black monarch, rival of Mutesa, named Kabba Rega. By this time Gordon had such an abysmal opinion of the Egyptian soldier that he was hardly surprised to find that, in spite of all the reports he had had of a successful occupation, the so-called garrison had never been nearer than 40 miles to Masindi, but had from the beginning established themselves in a hide-out where they had been left unmolested. 'Poor creatures. You cannot expect better' was his only comment.

. On returning to Magungo, he was faced with an embarrassing situation. Delighted by the report of Mutesa's submission, the Khedive sent a letter congratulating Gordon on his brilliant achievement, and conferring on him the much coveted decoration, the Order of Medjidieh, First Class. Gordon thought it 'dreadful', but showed an unusual flash of humour when he noted in his diary 'I am glad His Highness is pleased, though it is for an event which has not taken place.' Probably at the time he was thinking of his remark to Emin — 'Mutesa has annexed my soldiers, not been annexed himself. . .'

But it was the last straw. From Magungo he made his way up to Lado where he boarded a steamer for Khartoum.

Gordon was eagerly looking forward to being back in England. He wrote to Augusta 'I want oysters when I come home, and lots of them, not a dozen but four dozen. . .' His great problem, however, on the leisurely river journey was whether or not he would agree to return to Equatoria. It was not simply a question of his own wishes in the matter. He submitted himself to a severe cross-examination. Had he or had he not performed the duties with which he had been entrusted? Even with his miserable troops he had curbed the slave trade. Enormous numbers of slaves had been liberated — though what, he kept asking himself, was their future as officially free men? And the improvement, he saw, could only be temporary, for Cairo, while paying lip service to anti-slave sentiments, was far too involved in the profitable 'black ivory' traffic to wish for its total suppression. He could also claim that he had succeeded in exploring Lake Albert, and had solved the vexed question regarding the source of the Nile, but he had not extended the Khedive's authority, and both Mutesa and Kabba Rega could still proclaim themselves lords of all they surveyed. Compared with the years in China, if one judged by results, he had barely earned his salary!

These thoughts so depressed him that by the time Cairo was reached he was in a thoroughly belligerent mood. As soon as he met Ismail, he declared that he was leaving Egypt for good. The Khedive had other ideas. Exercising all his famous charm, he was able to mollify Gordon. He, he vowed, would redouble his efforts to crush the slavers if, in return, Gordon would promise to carry on his governorship as soon as his health was restored.

It may be that Gordon was happy to have his mind made up for him. In any case the two men parted the best of friends, Gordon giving his solemn promise that he would be back in a few months.

Being nearer home, events in Egypt made more impact on the English public than those in China, and on arrival at Southampton, Gordon found himself very much the man of the moment. 'What if he had accomplished next to nothing of practical value? He had carried himself like an Englishman, daring all, fearing nothing, rising from discouragement after discouragement, to face fearful odds with a smile and a quotation from the Bible. . .'

But he was not prepared to be an object of adulation. Invitations were stubbornly refused. As if nothing had happened he went back to the hermit-like existence which was the rule under Augusta's roof. He had promised himself dozens of oysters and the luxury of staying in bed till lunch time. It is doubtful if he ever realised these essentially innocent relaxations. Staying in bed till lunchtime would have meant missing nine o'clock family prayers, and pandering to such a thing as a craving for oysters a horrible example of yielding to the desires of the flesh.

This time, however, public opinion was not prepared to allow the hero of the day to slip back into oblivion; there would never be another Gravesend. Soon *The Times* was demanding that the ex-Governor of Equatoria was obviously the ideal man to fit the post of Governor of Bulgaria, a country just freed from Turkish domination. The idea held great appeal for Gordon. When he was summoned to the Foreign Office to discuss its possibilities, he was so carried away by enthusiasm that he sent off a hurried note to the

Khedive to say that he would not, after all, be returning to Egypt. He was anticipating over-optimistically.

The European Powers were not prepared to see a mere English colonel virtual king of Bulgaria. His name was ignored, and to add to his dilemma, towards the end of January (1877) he received a letter from Ismail reminding him of their last conversation.

'My dear Gordon,

I was astonished yesterday to hear from Monsieur Vivian (British Consul-General in Cairo) of a despatch you had sent him saying you would not come back, particularly as I recall our understanding at the Abdin Palace about completing the work we had begun together. So I must attribute your telegram to the entirely natural sentiments now that you are back home amongst your friends, but, my dear Gordon Pasha, I am unable to believe that a gentleman like Gordon could go back upon a solemn promise, and so I await your return.

Your affectionate

Ismail.

The Khedive had caught Gordon on his tenderest spot; his pride in his pledged word. Though the post in Bulgaria had failed to materialize, he was still unwilling to be re-employed by Ismail whom he liked as a man but distrusted as a ruler. In desperation he conceived the idea of imposing such an impossible condition, that the Khedive would be bound to refuse. Certain that his scheme would work, he left England after telling everyone that he would be back within a few weeks.

The moment he set foot in Cairo, he asked to see the Prime Minister's secretary, and through him delivered what was more or less an ultimatum. It was to the effect that he, Gordon, was not prepared to reoccupy the subordinate position of Governor of Equatoria. He must be given the whole of the Sudan, replacing Ayoub Pasha whom once again he accused of sabotaging all serious efforts to crush the slavers.

To his utter amazement, bordering on dismay, Ismail accepted without hesitation. Instead of arranging a passage back to England, Gordon found himself Governor General of the Sudan and of the ex-Abyssinian provinces of Harar and Berbera, and Marshal of the Egyptian army.

5

Lord of the Sudan

Lt. Colonel Gordon of the Royal Engineers, whose salary in England commanding a depot in some such place as Chatham would have been a bare £1,000 a year, was now lord and master of an area twice the size of western Europe entitled to a salary of £12,000 a year — which true to form he had demanded be reduced to £6,000 — limitless allowances, and the power to pass any law and prescribe any punishment.

Despite the constant nagging fear that ambition was sinful, the prospect of being able to bring civilization, according to his ideas, to this considerable slice of Africa excited him. His mood, once he had recovered from his astonishment, was well expressed in one of his first letters to Augusta: 'To give your life to be taken at once is one thing; to live such a life as is before me is another and more trying ordeal. I have set my face to this work and will give my life for it. I am only very slightly elated by the honours and power given me. I feel sure of success, for I do not lean on my own understanding and He directs my path. . .'

No time was wasted in Cairo, but before officially taking up residence in his capital, Khartoum, Gordon was asked to carry out a delicate diplomatic mission to King Johannes of Abyssinia, to try to arrange peace, or at least a truce, between him and a tribal chief, Walad el Michael, raiding into Abyssinia from Egyptian-held territory. The negotiations were never concluded. Walad el Michael agreed to every suggestion Gordon put foward, without having the slightest intention of ever keeping his word, while Johannes sent a message that threats in other parts of his kingdom, demanding his presence, made it impossible for him to meet the Khedive's envoy. Gordon solved the problem — at least to his own satisfaction — by drawing up a treaty, signing it himself and sending it to Johannes with a note that unless he heard to the contrary within a reasonable lapse of time, he would take it for granted that the King was in complete agreement.

Due to his horror of wasting time on a journey, Gordon arrived in Khartoum before expected. He was surprised to find hurried repairs being carried out on the Governor-General's palace, a building 'as big as Marlborough House' he noted, under the supervision of frightened officials.

Ayoub Pasha himself had taken his dismissal calmly. Not so his sister, who, in a fit of rage, had made a systematic tour of the vast edifice, smashing windows and ripping upholstery. It was a subtle revenge, for, as Gordon soon discovered, 'there was hardly another pane of glass in the country, still less suitable fabric to repair the divans'. Nor was the idea of an 'infidel' ruler popular with the city's inhabitants, and when he rode through the gates, the streets were almost deserted.

It was not long, however, before this hostility changed to near worship.

Gordon always believed in the efficacy of deeds rather than words. His initial speech broke all records for brevity — 'With God's help, I will hold the balance level.' But this somewhat obscure phrase was followed by a series of laws and decrees aimed at improving the lot of the poor, who formed the vast majority of his subjects.

Such normal practices of the past as torture by the police and public bastinadoing, were rigorously forbidden. One sixth of the privy purse was devoted to poor relief. Anyone with a grievance was invited to submit a petition. All these measures left officials badly shaken, but they were completely shattered — as was every individual no matter what his status — when it was announced that bribery was to be abolished. They could not take it seriously at first. The white man might be mad, they argued, but surely not as mad as all that, for if bribery were to be done away with, why had he accepted the post of Governor-General? To begin with, we are told 'every petitioner handed in his bribe, and when Gordon handed it back burst into sobs, imagining that his petition had been rejected. . .'

Though Gordon was by then attuned to the local character, he was never able to curb his irritation at the tortuous meanderings of the oriental mind, and was delighted when an uprising gave him the excuse to get away from the capital and its many administrative problems.

The province known as Darfur lay to the south west, a vast expanse of desert bordering Chad. There the Khedive's authority was upheld by Egyptian recruited troops known as Bashi-Bazouks, scattered over the country in isolated posts. Ill-paid, always short of supplies, they were in the habit of pillaging villages and rustling sheep and goats not so much from natural predatory instincts, but to avoid starvation. These raids did not endear them to the locals, either sedentary or nomadic, and at the time of Gordon's investiture, the Darfur garrisons found themselves pinned down by marauding bands, who in addition to refusing to pay Egyptian taxes, were constantly raiding the more lonely garrisons.

To put down this revolt of well over 5,000 tough

tribesmen, led by Haroun, son of the ex-Sultan of Darfur who had been murdered on Ismail's orders, Gordon set out at the head of 500 soldiers whom he described as 'nondescript'. Once again he was gambling on the force of his personality and example to inspire the rabble under his command, and as he was already beginning to feel an affinity for the desert tribes, he remarked 'I sincerely hope not to have to fire a shot in this revolt. The poor people have been driven into it. . .'

To make sure that there could be no doubt amongst the dissidents that it was Gordon Pasha in person leading the expedition, he rode his camel well ahead of his men, dressed in his full marshal's regalia; a gorgeous scarlet uniform smothered with gold braid.

'I go up alone' he said, an allusion to the poor quality of his troops 'with Almighty God to direct and guide me, and am glad to so trust Him as to fear nothing and, indeed, feel sure of success. . .'

His faith was completely justified. Within three months the rebellion was over. He had ridden to the relief of besieged post after besieged post. The sight of the scarlet clad figure indifferent to danger had the desired effect. As he had hoped, hardly a shot was fired. Nor was there any talk of indemnity, let alone acts of reprisal. The head of each tribe or village was brought to Gordon personally and asked to detail his grievances. Where possible legitimate grievances were remedied on the spot. The only people who suffered during these operations were his own men whom, as usual, he exhausted by the tremendous distances he insisted on covering daily — on one occasion 85 miles in 36 hours — so that by the time he could claim that the situation was in hand, he had ridden the best part of 3,000 miles in three months.

In between relieving besieged posts, he had taken the opportunity to beard many of the slavers in their lairs. 'He arrived out of the blue, broke in on the slavers and demanded their submission to the government in his person. While they were fingering their daggers or their revolvers menacingly, he would turn his back on them to light a cigarette; then wheel round puffing equably, to fix them with a hard blue eye or dumbfound them with a boyish grin. His Arabic was so atrocious that they, too, had to smile. . .'

It is a miracle that he lived so long, that some knife—or trigger— happy Sudanese did not succumb to what must have been a great temptation. The answer was that they admired him. Had he blustered, hesitated, or shown any sign of fear he would probably have been killed on the spot. So, between them and Gordon there came into being what in later years would have been termed a gentleman's agreement. Added to this was the fact that the more he saw of the desert people, the more he preferred them to the Egyptians to whom he owed loyalty. 'I like the slave dealers' he wrote candidly 'they are a brave lot, and putting aside propensities to take slaves, are much finer people than those of lower Egypt. Would *you* shoot them all? Do you know cargoes of slaves came into British harbours in the time of our fathers? When in 1834 H.M.G. abolished slavery, they had an irresistible force with fleets, troops etc. at their disposal . . . In my case I have nothing of the sort. . .'

Toughest, and most powerful of the slavers with whom Gordon had to deal was Suliman, son of Zubehr, the Black Khedive. At the time Zubehr was in a Cairo gaol, having been lured treacherously to the capital to talk over the possibility of some sort of agreement with the Khedive.

Suliman commanded three thousand battle-tried Sudanese warriors. Yet once again the appearance of the scarlet-uniformed rider, so far ahead of his men as to be virtually alone, impressed the cut-throat bodyguard to such an extent that they stood respectfully to attention when Gordon dismounted and, ignoring them, strode up to Suliman's tent and ordered him to report the following morning to Dar, the nearest Egyptian-held post. All Gordon had to say of the dreaded Suliman was — 'Nice looking lad, clearly a spoilt child who would be all the better for a spanking' adding 'Poor little chap. How bitter for him to be suddenly nothing after having been accustomed to do exactly what he liked, even to killing people. . .'

Though, as he admitted, Gordon was 'worn to a shadow' by the time he was back in Khartoum, he could not bear to stay long surrounded by the etiquette and ceremony incumbent on his position, and guarded, as he put it, 'like an ingot of gold'. Irritation and inactivity invariably brought on one of his moods, aggravated by the fact that, as in Equatoria, he doubted whether Egyptian rule could ever really benefit its heterogenous subjects.

Describing the unfortunate effect this combination of worries had on him, one of Gordon's staff noted that 'His temper grew uncontrollable. He kicked his frightened orderlies, growled at his visitors, shouted at the trail of impecunious, diseased men and women who followed him in the streets "I am more miserable than you".' He was overjoyed when at last he was able to plead the excuse of trouble on the Abyssinian border to substitute physical for mental trials, and indulge in his foible of reducing himself, his staff, and his escort to a state of collapse from utter fatigue.

He still hoped to meet the Abyssinian king. But whether Johannes feared he might fall to Gordon's powers of persuasion, or whether he was not even prepared to discuss any questions with Ismail's representative is not clear. The fact remains that he ignored all Gordon's invitations, attempts at cajolment, and veiled threats. The meeting on which Gordon had set so much store never materialised. Frustrated, he returned to Khartoum where he received an urgent call to go to Cairo to play a major role in an affair little to his liking, and with which he was totally unsuited to deal.

By February 1878, Ismail was in dire financial straits. In a few years Egypt's national debt had increased from three and a half to ninety-four million pounds sterling. At the same time he was himself a compulsive spender and in 1875 to appease creditors had sold Egypt's share in the Suez Canal for four million pounds. By 1876, he was forced to accept foreign control of Egyptian finances in the form of two Controllers-General, an Englishman Mr. Romane, and a Frenchman Baron de Mailleret, with another Englishman, Major Evelyn Baring (later Lord Cromer) as the Controllers-Generals' representative on the Commission of Debts.

Ismail, understandably, bitterly resented this foreign interference, but conditions in the country were growing daily more chaotic. The *fellahin* were submitted to every form of brutality by tax collectors. Lower-ranking officials seldom received their pay. To make matters worse, serious famine broke out in 1877. The Khedive, however, seized on this disaster as an excuse to suspend payments, and then, pursuing his delaying tactics, managed to obtain agreement for an international court of inquiry on Egypt's finances to be set up with Gordon as its president.

Gordon's appointment was not popular. Almost as soon as he arrived in Cairo, he was quarrelling with his fellow Englishmen who took the first opportunity of reminding him that his loyalty was to his own country, to which he replied that, on the contrary, it was to the man who employed him, the Khedive. He took a violent personal dislike to Major Baring whom he accused of being nothing but a 'pretty black-eyed boy who couldn't stand up to the R.M.A's tough routine' and 'pretentious'.

No politician, and certainly no financier, Gordon soon found himself completely at sea, continuing to quarrel ineffectually with everybody, and showing little grasp of the fact that the issues at stake were not of domestic, but of international significance. Ismail was one of the first to realise his mistake. He now saw quite clearly that his only hope of retaining his throne was to accept the role of European puppet. Very embarrassed, it was two days before he could pluck up the courage to tell Gordon that he was not the man to clean up the mess of Egyptian finances, that de Lesseps — of Suez Canal fame — would act as president to a freshly composed court, and that he had engaged the services of a British financial adviser, Rivers Wilson. 'His Highness was bored with me after my failure' Gordon commented bitterly 'and could not bear the sight of me'.

Within a fortnight of his arrival, he was on his way back to Khartoum, glad to be free of Cairo's intrigues, yet deeply resentful of the way he had been treated not only by his fellow countrymen, and especially Baring, but by the master to whom he had given such total fidelity, the Khedive Ismail. As he paced the steamer's deck staring out over the featureless desert, a sense of having been disgraced and ridiculed prompted him to note in his diary 'Of all the countries of the earth, I can imagine none so detestable to govern as Egypt'. And even before the steamer docked at Khartoum, he had composed a letter to the War Office requesting to be re-employed by Her Majesty's Government; a letter which was never answered.

Once in Khartoum, it seemed that Gordon's phenomenal energy had been drained from him. For six months, he never stirred outside the walls, devoting himself to administrative and financial problems. The latter were thorny. The Sudan was over £300,000 in the red, and after the Khedive's capitulation to the European bankers, Gordon was constantly nagged by queries and suggestions from both Baring and Rivers Wilson. To bring some measure of relief to the strained budget, he made two suggestions himself both of which were acted upon and were to have a profound influence on history. They were that the Red Sea provinces of Berbera and Harar be sold to Italy, and that work on the railway to link Wadi Halfa with Khartoum be abandoned. The sale of the Red Sea provinces gave Italy her foothold in East Africa, laying the foundation of the expansionist policy culminating in Mussolini's seizure of Abyssinia in 1936, prelude to the second world war, while suspension of the work on the railway can be considered one of the major factors responsible for the failure of the relief column to arrive in time to save Gordon himself from Dervish spears.

As well as the growing worry of trying to make both ends meet, there was further trouble from Suliman, again defying authority and rapidly making a fortune in 'black ivory' encouraged in his activities by Gordon's apparent inertia. At the head of an army swelled to close on 10,000 and acquiring a reputation for ruthless cruelty seldom equalled even in Africa, he overran a number of Egyptian posts, and was threatening to set up an independent kingdom of Darfur. At the same time, from his cell in a Cairo gaol, his father, the 'Black Khedive' Zubehr, was bargaining for his freedom with an offer of yearly payments of £25,000 and the promise that if he were sent as emissary to Suliman peace would be restored immediately.

Gordon, who remarked that the young man he had once described as a 'cub' had now grown into a 'dangerous wolf', reacted swiftly. He had captured correspondence from Zubehr urging his son to revolt and thus proving that he was the actual instigator of the rebellion. Letting Cairo know that if Zubehr set foot in Sudanese territory he would hang him, he got to work to organize a punitive expedition that would smash Suliman before the situation could be further complicated by the Khedive.

Though he would have preferred to head the expedition, Gordon felt that his presence in the capital to counter any subversive moves was essential. Against his will, therefore, command of the 2,500 strong column which left Khartoum towards the end of July was entrusted to Romolo Gessi.

Weeks of marching and counter marching followed, but it was not till December that a major clash occurred when as a result of a surprise night attack one of Suliman's main bases was taken. Though heavily outnumbered, Gessi, who had absorbed much of Gordon's genius as a leader as well as a large measure of his outstanding courage under fire, was anxious to bring Suliman to battle. The setback, he hoped, would goad the slaver into committing his whole force in an attempt to recapture the camp. His appreciation was correct, and he was able to meet Suliman's main assault from behind hastily prepared, but well sited defensive positions. Suliman's men were brave, but ill led. Decimated as they charged over open ground, they broke, leaving a third of their number dead or dying littering the ground in front of the Egyptian stockades and trenches. Suliman himself and his bodyguard fled.

Hearing of this success, Gordon decided to get away from Khartoum and visit Gessi on the scene of his victory. A message was sent fixing a rendezvous at Shakka, most important of the Egyptian garrisons in the Darfur; a distance of 340 miles. During the march he was afforded melancholy proof of the precarious state of his health and the deterioration of his physical condition. Even though it was mid winter, the heat was too much for him. At the end of each day's march he was ready to drop. He suffered not only from a congested liver, but a series of minor heart attacks.

En route several slave caravans were intercepted. The slavers caught were lucky to escape execution. But though he admitted that he would have liked to have had them shot summarily, Gordon was not prepared to contravene the law of his own making which laid down that the penalty for trading in slaves — as opposed to actually taking them — was five years imprisonment. Nevertheless, he was determined to teach them such a lesson, that those who survived five years in an Eygptian gaol would not be tempted to renew their activities. After being given a beating guaranteed to scar them for life, they were loaded with chains and marched to Khartoum, a march which a number failed to complete.

The meeting between Gordon and his most reliable

lieutenant took place early in January 1879. Gessi was full of confidence. Suliman was a fugitive and all his attempts to induce other tribes to take up arms had failed. The Italian had matters so well in hand that Gordon, always afraid that Zubehr might turn up unexpectedly armed with a safe conduct bearing Ismail's signature, decided to return to his capital after congratulating Gessi and assuring him that in the event of Suliman falling into his hands, *whatever decision he cared to make,* would receive his chief's blessing.

Three weeks later, accompanied by the pick of his escort, a bare 250 men, acting on information from locals who in the past had been victims of the slavers depradations, Gessi caught up with Suliman when the latter was hiding by night in a remote village. Though he knew that his prey had at least a thousand well armed desperate men with him, Gessi sent in a messenger at dawn to announce that the village was surrounded, that resistance was useless, and calling for immediate surrender. The bluff worked. The bodyguard laid down their arms without firing a shot, and Suliman gave himself up with ten of his principal henchmen.

The exact circumstances of the sequel are open to speculation. According to Gessi, he received reliable information the following night that the eleven prisoners were planning a break-away. He could not, he said, accept the risk of such an eventuality. Armed therefore with Gordon's verbal promise to back any on-the-spot decision he might be forced to take, he ordered the eleven men to be dragged from their tents and shot. Gordon heard the news with a sigh of relief, and there is no record of his pressing Gessi for precise details concerning the supposed escape plan.

The Italian's success convinced him that as many non-Egyptians as possible should be included in the Sudanese government. Gessi was made governor of Bahr-el-Ghazal, a former slaver stronghold. Emin, the German turned Moslem who had rescued Nuehr Agha from Mutesa's clutches, became governor of Equatoria. An English merchant navy officer,

Frank Lupton, was taken on as personal assistant, and a young Austrian cavalry officer, Rudolf Carl von Slatin, recommended by Emin, was sent to Darfur. So long as he remained in the saddle, Gordon was certain that with such a team he could reduce the slave trade to a minimum even if he could not stamp it out altogether. But though satisfied that at last all was well in the Sudan, he was becoming more and more convinced that his efforts were being systematically sabotaged by Cairo.

From various sources of information, he calculated that in a year roughly four hundred slave caravans had headed north to Egypt from black Africa. He himself had intercepted sixty-eight; what had the Egyptians done about the rest? He could only conclude that profits from 'black ivory' were being used to subsidize government salaries. In a formal complaint he stated 'Whenever a caravan escapes from the Sudan to Egypt it is safe. How many caravans have been captured in Egypt against the caravans I have captured in the Sudan? I do not believe that one has. . .'

The complaint was ignored. Once more Gordon wrote a furious letter to the Khedive asking to be relieved from his post.

Ismail countered by asking Gordon to come to Cairo to discuss the matter. Gordon, afraid that he would not be strong enough to resist should Ismail turn on his noted charm, prevaricated. There was nothing to discuss, he wrote back; his mind was made up.

The argument dragged on but was never concluded. In the end Gordon remained in Khartoum. It was Ismail who left Cairo.

In spite of European advisers, Egyptian finances were still in the most dire straits. Ismail could not even cope with the interest let alone reduce the capital borrowed. A sale of crown land, a million acres for eight and a half million pounds, brought no relief. An attempt to cut down on national expenditure by arbitrarily retiring two thousand three hundred army officers without making up long overdue arrears of pay, came near to sparking off a mutiny, only prevented after the Khedive had given a promise that 'eventually' the arrears would be paid and some form of gratuity voted. Thinking that he could turn this embryo mutiny to his own advantage, Ismail informed the European powers that it was in fact a protest against foreign interference in Egypt's internal affairs, and to add substance to this statement, dismissed his two advisers, Rivers Wilson and de Blignières, replacing them by Egyptians.

Britain and France reacted vigorously, at the same time procuring a powerful ally, the Prussian Otto von Bismark, the 'Iron Chancellor', very much the strong man of Europe. Bismark, who believed in bullying and intimidation, suggested that protests worded so strongly that they were virtually ultimatums should be despatched immediately. As a result two documents were despatched bearing Britain and France's joint signatures, the one to Ismail suggesting 'voluntary' abdication, the other to the Turkish Sultan, stating that if he did not wish the matter to be taken out of his hands, he had better issue the necessary decree deposing the present Khedive and appointing a successor.

The Sultan, perfectly aware of the fact that but for Britain and France, Turkey would be swallowed up by Russia, did not hesitate. The same day a telegram was sent to Cairo addressed to the 'ex-Khedive', informing him that he was to abdicate immediately in favour of his son Tewfik.

Gordon received the news with surprising indifference. It affected him only, he wrote, in so much as it made him wonder whether he ought not to stay on at his post in the hope that the new ruler would prove less venal and less incompetent than his predecessor. After days of doubts, fears, changes of mind, all recorded in his letters, he decided suddenly that no improvement could be expected since

Tewfik was 'a miserable creature' and that his resignation must stand. He did agree, however, to meet the new Khedive when he arrived in Cairo on August 22nd.

Tewfik had inherited something of his father's charm. After their first encounter Gordon temporarily forgot that he had referred to him as a 'miserable creature' writing instead that he was 'a man of talent, energy, and the manner of the "Incurable" (a contemptuous nickname for Ismail) but with a quality the latter did not possess, i.e., honesty. . .'

In spite of this change of opinion, Gordon was not prepared to countermand his resignation, but after a series of talks agreed to carry out one last task for Egypt; to make a third effort to meet King Johannes of Abyssinia and draw up a treaty which would put an end to the semi-permanent state of insecurity existing on both sides of the Egypt-Abyssinian frontier.

King Johannes, also known as the Ras Tafari (King of Kings) and Lion of Judah was bigoted and sadistic. If one of his subjects were discovered taking snuff, he was liable to have his nose cut off. For comparatively minor offences, a man could have his ears filled with boiling candle grease which had the effect of making him not only incurably deaf, but blind. In addition he suffered from megalomania. He regarded himself as the equal, if not the superior, of any European monarch, and this despite the fact that he was barely literate, and lived in a so-called palace made of two round huts, windowless and doorless. As to his personal habits, Gordon was fond of saying that 'he was psalm singing every morning and drunk every night. . .'

Nor was the Abyssinian monarch an easy man to find. Gordon was obliged to undertake a series of long and tiring journeys before at last catching up with him. It was not worth the trouble. Gordon took an instant dislike to the 'sour ill-looking being', as he described him, and made no attempt to disguise his sentiments. For the meeting to have had any chance of success, Gordon should have recognized the fact that Johannes was half mad, and adopted a tactful, quasi-conciliatory approach. Instead, exhausted both mentally and physically, he could not have been in a more aggressive, cantankerous mood and rather than humouring his host's idiosyncracies, appeared determined to give offence.

He had already discovered that Johannes looked upon smoking as a deadly sin, yet he walked into the King of Kings presence puffing at a cigar. Johannes was sitting cross legged on a throne made of three benches piled one on top of the other swaddled in white silk robes, his Ministers squatting on the floor like 'white cocoons'. In the far right hand corner was a small wooden chair. This, the interpreter told Gordon, was for him. Ignoring the remark, Gordon walked across the room, picked the chair up, carried it close to the throne and sat down. No sooner had he made this openly defiant gesture than he informed the King that, being invested with ambassadorial status by the Khedive of Egypt, he must be treated as an equal, otherwise there would be no discussion.

The enraged Johannes told Gordon very forcibly that he would be within his rights if he ordered his instant execution for such impertinence.

'I am always ready to die,' Gordon replied coldly, 'And so far from fearing your putting me to death, you would confer on me a favour by so doing, for you would be doing for me that which I am precluded by my religious scruples from doing for myself — you would relieve me of all the troubles and misfortunes which the future may have in store for me.'

Astonished, Johannes asked — 'Then my powers mean nothing to you?' To which Gordon replied 'Nothing!'

After this inauspicious opening, an attempt was made to discuss the business in hand. Johannes began by presenting his demands; a stretch of the Red Sea coast including a port, and a 'peace offering' from Egypt of two million pounds. With undiplomatic brusqueness, Gordon told him he was talking nonsense, adding that if he persisted with 'such folly',

Egypt would arm Abyssinia's enemies. This reply provoked another storm of abuse, ended only when Gordon told 'the ugly little man' that he was not the Almighty, and the sooner he realised the fact, the better it would be for him. Gordon's manner, his choice of words, were altogether so insulting, that one cannot help wondering whether, obsessed as he was by his death wish, he were not trying deliberately to provoke Johannes into committing murder.

However, the King of Kings managed to control his temper — perhaps for the first time in his life — and declared the interview at an end. Twelve days passed before he would agree to a second meeting. This put Gordon into such a rage that the moment he was shown into Johannes's presence, he opened the proceedings by demanding the instant and unconditional release of all Egyptian prisoners, following this with a suggestion that the ban on smoking should be lifted. This was too much for Johannes who promptly ordered Gordon to leave the country with the least possible delay.

The hoped for peace conference was ended! The fault, it must be admitted, as much Gordon's as that of the half-mad Johannes.

The return journey in the bitter cold of the Abyssinian highlands was prolonged by an incident which might have proved fatal.

Shortly after setting out, Gordon and his escort were held up by Abyssinian troops. After being robbed of most of his personal possessions he was marched off 'on the King's orders' to the nearest gaol and kept under close arrest, seven men on permanent guard over him, and bitten to death by every known form of bug. There is no doubt that the outraged Johannes was debating whether or not to make an example of the insolent foreigner despite the protection normally afforded by diplomatic status.

It would have been in keeping with his character had he done so. But again Gordon was lucky. After a few days, orders were received for all the prisoners to be released, and the journey was resumed, the danger of frost-bite being added to the many hazards of the road.

Eventually the exhausted little column reached the port of Massawa. There Gordon had the good fortune to find the British gunboat *Seagull* on which he was able to travel as far as Suez, where he boarded the Cairo train. Before reporting the failure of his mission to the Khedive, he procured a medical certificate from the Embassy doctor to the effect that he was in such a poor state of health that 'several months' complete rest and quiet and total exemption from all exacting work especially such as implies business or political excitement' was essential.

Because his nerves and temper were so worn, Gordon unjustly reversed his original favourable impressions of the young Khedive, even going as far as to blame him — rather than his own lamentable lack of tact — for the breakdown of the talks with Johannes. In a letter he stated 'From the start I knew instinctively that Tewfik was false' and went on to suggest that he had been sent on this hopeless mission because the Khedive counted on the fact that 'if violence were done to his (Gordon's) person, then Britain would join in actively with Egypt in her dispute with Abyssinia. . .'

The whole month spent in Cairo before leaving Egypt and Africa 'for ever' as he imagined was fully occupied by a succession of quarrels with everyone he encountered. He was in the habit of saying openly that 'the new Khedive is an idiot and not fit to rule.' Though it was repeated to him, Tewfik preferred to turn a deaf ear, contenting himself with sending Gordon a cold, formal letter, on the eve of his departure, thanking him for his services to Egypt.

Gordon sailed in the latter half of February. There was no official send-off. His own farewell was a remark which he knew would be widely publicized — 'I do not profess to have been a great ruler, or a great financier, but I can say this — I have cut off the slave dealers in their strongholds and I made the people love me. . .'

6

The Years of Indecision

The year 1880 was a difficult one for the ex-Governor of the Sudan. His ship was barely out of sight of the Egyptian coast, before he was reproaching himself for abandoning *his* people to the mercies of the Pashas. But his principal grudge was against life itself and the cruelty of Destiny which kept him on earth when all he longed for was to be 'on high' with his Maker. The world, he kept on writing, was a detestable place and man an equally detestable animal.

In no hurry to reach England, he travelled slowly via Athens, Constantinople, Naples and Rome, in the Italian capital striking up a friendship with a Frenchman, a Monsieur Reinach, a sympathetic listener who spent most of his time being verbally overwhelmed by Gordon's bitter attacks on rulers and politicians, in particular and in general, and his grandiose schemes for righting existing wrongs and substituting an era of peace and plenty for the present era of greed, corruption, and belligerence. The few occasions when he attempted to take his friend's mind off his grievances by showing him some of the natural and man-made beauties of the country, Monsieur Reinach had to admit failure. Gordon was not interested in natural or architectural beauty; worse, they depressed and irritated him. As for the arts, they were lumped together under the general heading 'sinful'. The Naples opera to which he was dragged most unwillingly, he qualified as 'ungodly rubbish'. At the end of the first act he 'could stand no more of it', and walked out.

In England, he was unable to retire immediately to the hermitage of Rockstone Place. To his horror he found that once again, he was headline material. He could not avoid attending a levée at Buckingham Palace, but refused an invitation to dine with the Prince of Wales.

When the equerry suggested that one just did *not* refuse such invitations, Gordon's answer was — 'Why not. I refused King Johannes and he might have cut off my head for refusing. I am sure His Royal Highness will not do that.'

'Then let me say you are ill.'

'But I am not ill.'

'Then give me some reason I can give the Prince.'

'Very well then — tell him I always go to bed at half past nine!'

The Prince's reaction was to issue an invitation to lunch, which Gordon had the grace to accept.

As soon as possible, however, he had shut himself up in Southampton despite the fact that the formidable Augusta still refused to allow her famous brother to indulge in his passion for smoking other than late at night in the kitchen. However, this Spartan regime did nothing to restore his much impaired health, and finally his doctors, worried by his lack of progress, advised a trip to Switzerland. Secretly he was not sorry to have a legitimate excuse to get away.

He travelled via Belgium, the Brussels visit being prompted by a renewal of ambition's itch, which in spite of his horror of temporal power, he was never able to suppress. While in London, his friend of the long past Crimean days,

Sir Garnet Wolseley, had introduced him to the King of the Belgians, a meeting which engendered a wildly romantic idea.

Belgium had just taken over a vast area of the Congo, an area known to produce one of the world's most flourishing slave harvests. This presented him with an unique chance to finish the work begun in the Sudan. He would resign his commission in the British army, enter the service of the Belgian King, race to the Congo, and there deal the slavers a death blow. His enthusiasm, however, was not shared either by Sir Garnet or by that shrewd judge of men, the Prince of Wales. Both felt that though Gordon was a most difficult individual, he was a soldier of genius who could be ill-spared by his own country.

Though agreeing, grudgingly, to think matters over before taking a step which could prove irrevocable, Gordon refused to abandon the idea and was hoping that a further meeting with King Leopold would result in a firm offer to launch him on the anti-slaver crusade. Nothing concrete seems to have emerged from their talks, though it is probable Gordon gave his word that provided he could get British government permission, he would be off to the Congo as soon as was humanly possible.

From Brussels, he went straight to Lausanne where he made the acquaintance of an Anglican clergyman, the Reverend R.H.Barnes. The chance meeting developed into a life friendship. Mr. Barnes was so impressed by his new found friend's 'Godliness', that he compared him and 'his distaste for the body, his longing for death' with a 'mediaeval mystic'. The days in Lausanne were passed in interminable conversations — with Gordon as usual doing most of the talking — and before parting the two men agreed to keep up a regular correspondence. They kept their word, and from then on Gordon's letters to the rectory of the Devonshire parish of Heavitree were as frequent as those to Rockstone Place.

Shortly after his return to England, Gordon was delighted

by the fall of the conservative government, especially as one
of the new appointments of the liberals was that of his old
friend Sir Garnet, now Lord Wolseley, to the War Office as
Adjutant General. He had always blamed Disraeli for not
taking Egyptian problems seriously enough, being lukewarm
in his attitude to the slave trade's suppression, and though
basically apolitical himself, was more in sympathy with Whig
than Tory principles. He was not mistaken in thinking that he
was more likely to be offered a job by the Gladstone than the
Disraeli administration, but the post eventually offered him
in September 1880 — that of Private Secretary to the new
Viceroy of India, Lord Ripon — was one totally unsuited to a
man of his views and temperament. It is difficult to
understand how anyone could have imagined his filling such
a role; still more difficult to understand why he accepted the
appointment, and with evident enthusiasm.

For all his hankering after humility, Gordon was
accustomed to giving, not receiving, orders, a man who all his
life had avoided any form of sedentary occupation like the
plague, only relaxed on active service, the only music sweet
on his ears that of the guns. These uncompromising facets of
his nature were fully understood in War Office circles.
Everyone, including Gordon himself, concerned with this
appointment was equally fully aware that a secretary — even
Private Secretary to the Viceroy — would never be in a
position to issue an independent order, and that basic duties
would consist very largely in the fulfilment of social activities
in the very surroundings which he had always been at such
pains to avoid. In fact Gordon the Private Secretary provided
the perfect example of the metaphor 'A square peg in a
round hole.'

That the whole business was a ghastly mistake was
realised by both Gordon and his master long before their ship
docked at Bombay. From Aden, Gordon was writing to his
brother 'I shall get away as soon as I can do so in a
respectable manner' with the further comment 'I think it will

be no surprise to Lord Ripon who sees I am too truculent for the post. . .'

As was to be expected, the life of viceregal circles proved anathema. It was worse, far worse in Gordon's opinion, than Cairo, with its protocol, ceremonial, luxury, hosts of servants, eternal round of social events. From the whole melancholy experiment which, much to the relief of the interested parties, lasted only a few weeks, there is only one incident worth recording; an historic remark of great shrewdness made by Gordon during a discussion of the pros and cons of a further attempt to annex Afghanistan. In reply to the argument that such a poor, troubled, turbulent country would benefit vastly by enlightened Western rule, he remarked 'I cannot think that any people like being governed by aliens in race or religion. They prefer their own bad native governments to a stiff, civilized government, in spite of the increased worldly prosperity the latter may give. . .'

After this calamity Gordon was firmly convinced that he was unemployable in the British army, and in spite of hints that he was soon to be promoted General, was again clamouring to be allowed to resign his commission. He was on the point of applying for 'extended leave of absence' when he received a telegram from Shanghai from Sir Robert Hart, friend of his Ever Victorious Army days — 'I am directed to invite you to China. Please come and see for yourself. This opportunity for doing really useful work on a large scale ought not to be lost. Work, position, conditions can all be arranged with yourself here to your satisfaction. Do take six months' leave and come.'

Suspecting that it was his old friend Li who was the real instigator of the telegram, and the passing years having misted the memory of their many quarrels, Gordon replied immediately — 'Inform Hart Gordon will leave for Shanghai first opportunity. As for conditions Gordon indifferent.'

Next step was to satisfy a suspicious War Office that he

was not going to China to raise a private army and launch out in a series of adventures — possibly of an anti-Russian nature — which might prove embarrassing for international relationships. But at last, after a prolonged exchange of telegrams, the six months' leave was granted on the condition that he promised to 'take no military service in China.'

Leaving Bombay on 12 June, he arrived in Shanghai on 12 July to find himself plunged into the same whirlpool of intrigue he had left nearly twenty years ago. Not only did war with Russia seem imminent, but yet another civil war appeared to be brewing.

The job, Sir Robert Hart explained, involved diplomacy. Li was to be contacted and urged to cease his efforts to push China into a conflict with Russia. It was an important mission, for Li, heaped with decorations and titles — among them those of Senior Guardian of the Heir Apparent, Senior Grand Secretary, and wearer of the Double-Eyed Peacock's feather — was one of the most influential men in the country. Without wasting a moment Gordon set off up country.

Li made a tremendous fuss of his old friend — he, too, chose to push memories of disputes into the background — and Gordon was amazed to find that Sir Robert Hart had completely misunderstood the situation. Li agreed with Gordon that if it came to war, China would not stand a chance against the Russian army. He was totally opposed to the idea. The war party was in fact headed by Prince Chun, the boy emperor's father, who went so far as to qualify Li's pacificism as 'unpatriotic'. Gordon said he would go to Pekin.

In the Chinese capital he was cordially welcomed. He found that even Chun was prepared to listen and talk things over. On the other hand he soon fell out with the British Minister, Sir Thomas Wade. It was not really Sir Thomas's fault. The Foreign Office was worried by the presence in Pekin of the 'trouble-maker Gordon', and the Minister received the extraordinary order to put him 'under moral arrest'. He therefore sent for Gordon and told him that he was not to leave the British Legation's grounds without permission. Gordon, as was to be expected, was furious. Sending a telegram to the War Office demanding permission to resign his commission, at the same time he openly defied the order which Sir Thomas was powerless to enforce. And though he began to suspect that British secret policy was to see China involved in war with Russia which would automatically distract the latter's attention from Afghanistan and India, he continued to pester Prince Chun to give up his bellicose ideas.

His arguments, in support of those of Li, eventually bore fruit. The idea of war was dropped. Instead negotiations were opened to settle the current disputes which had brought the two vast countries to the verge of open hostilities.

His mission accomplished, Gordon decided suddenly that he did not wish to remain a moment longer than necessary in the country. He had squabbled with Li. Having helped to avoid war, he was full of grandiose and fanciful ideas for the remodelling of China and was anxious that Li should be his mouthpiece. Li, always a rabid conservative, was not prepared to listen. He saw no reason why China's age-old civilization, her millenary way of life, should change. Always infuriated by opposition, Gordon promptly accused Li of being 'weak and unreliable'. Their parting, though outwardly cordial, was at heart frigid.

Within five weeks of setting foot in China Gordon was on the high seas bound for England.

At Aden he was badly worried by a belated telegram from the War Office — 'Leave cancelled. Resignation not accepted.'

It placed him in an awkward situation. Overstaying leave laid any rank of the armed forces open to disciplinary action. He wired at once — 'You might have trusted me. My passage from China was taken days before the arrival of your telegram which states "leave cancelled" '. On arrival in England he wrote a long explanation stating among other things — 'I looked on war as so detrimental to China and England that any effort I could make would be cheaply bought at my personal sacrifice' to which the only reply was a grant of a further six months' leave.

Being a man who had no idea of the meaning of the word 'leisure', it was barely a month before Gordon was thoroughly restless and scanning the map of the world to try to discover some suitable, preferably uncivilized, spot where his pent-up energy could find an outlet. He was tempted by Zanzibar, always haunted by the thought of the slave trade, and wrote to the Sultan offering his services. The Sultan may have thought, or been warned, that Gordon's presence too often spelt trouble. In any case the letter was unanswered, and Gordon, keenly disappointed, made a much shorter journey — to Ireland.

By the time he had been a few days in the country, he was ready to take up the peasants' cause with all his usual fire.

'I must say' he wrote in a letter subsequently published in the Press 'that from all accounts and my own observation the state of our fellow countrymen in the parts I have named is worse than that of any people in the world, let alone Europe. I believe that these people are made as we are, that they are patient beyond belief, loyal, but at the same time broken-spirited and on the verge of starvation, living in places where we would not keep our cattle. . .'

After this and many other similar protests, he published his own solution; that 'on the precedent of buying out the slaves of the plantations, the Irish should be bought out of the hands of their English landlords. The landlords would be compensated and their vast properties become Crown land. This would be distributed to the peasants at government controlled rents, low enough for the individual family to live decently and make a little profit each year.'

Both the Home Office and the War Office, to say nothing

of the host of mainly absentee landlords, strongly disapproved of an army officer meddling in politics. It was
thought to be as well if Gordon could cool his ardour in some
far distant backwater. This was arranged by substituting
Gordon's name for that of an old Woolwich friend of his, Sir
Howard Elphinstone, in an appointment generally looked
upon as the most unpopular in the army; Commander of
Royal Engineers, Mauritius. Elphinstone himself had been so
appalled when he had heard his name mentioned that he had
been considering retirement rather than putting up with what
he termed 'being socially buried alive.'

Gordon accepted the post for two reasons. He was always
glad of an excuse to escape from the 'stifling atmosphere of
the British Isles', and also because after a revival of his
mysticism by a sudden 'revelation of the true meaning of
Holy Communion' he was sure that the posting was a
manifestation of God's will — 'I believe the pilgrimage to
Mauritius will be blessed to me, for I believe I was hanging
about Jordan, i.e. wishing for death and not caring to
conquer the promised land. . .'

Unfortunately, as had so often happened, he was incapable of maintaining his enthusiasm and 'acceptance' of
'God's will' when faced with a monotonous routine such as
that of garrison life on Mauritius. His command consisted of
only five other Royal Engineers, the entire garrison only
three troops of artillery and three companies of infantry. The
garrison commander, whose post Gordon felt at once
should have been offered to him, was General Murray, a
septuagenarian and rigidly conventional, with whom Gordon
had nothing in common.

Though stories of his eccentricities had preceded him,
Gordon was a national figure, and the small British
community looked forward to welcoming him as one of
them. He turned his back on their friendly overtures with a
brusqueness which could only be described as ill-mannered. 'I
strike against garden parties, archery and lawn tennis

meetings' he wrote to Mr. Barnes 'I cannot go through these fearful ordeals of hours' duration. . .' Not only did he persist in refusing all invitations, but when the white population moved up to the hills for the hot weather, he remained obstinately on the coast.

The troops were soon cursing the day he landed on their hitherto peaceful island. Till then idleness had been the keynote of life, and Gordon had reckoned that an hour a day was the maximum spent on parade. It was true that there was nothing useful they could do, but Gordon didn't care. He had them sweating on useless work of his own creation. As one officer said — 'He twirled them about like tops. They had no peace. Drills, parades, exercises, expeditions — their life was suddenly and unpleasantly full. . .'

In March 1882, came the expected promotion to Major-General, a step up which made him all the more eager to find a worthwhile employ. It was just as he was thinking of making another approach to the Sultan of Zanzibar that, to his surprise and delight, a cable arrived from the Cape Colony Government in South Africa, asking if he would be prepared to take over command of the Colony's forces. He cabled his acceptance by return.

The manner of his departure was in keeping with his reputation of social ogre. He walked twelve miles to a lonely spot on the coast where a rowing boat was waiting to take him to a sailing ship, the *Scotia,* on which he travelled to the Cape, so as to avoid any form of send-off.

The specific problem with which Gordon was expected to deal was the Basuto resistance to the Cape Government's authority. Because of constant Basuto raids, the Frontier between the Cape Colony and Basuto-land was a wasted no-man's-land, the scene of constant clashes for the last two years. An expedition mounted at the cost of over a million pounds had failed to crush the raiders.

On the surface it was just the sort of task at which

Gordon excelled. Yet his brief stay in the Cape was without doubt the most frustrating experience of his whole life. From the moment of his first interview with the South Africans in official positions, he disliked them as much as they disliked him. They could find no common ground of approach to the situation.

To begin with Gordon was really at heart a confirmed anti-colonialist. With him it was an automatic reflex to take the natives' part. His first comments were that 'the natives were goaded into rebellion by the badness and inefficiency of the magistracy'. In a memorandum dated 26 May 1882, he went on to say that 'in defiance of treaties the Basutos lost land' and that the disarmament demanded by the South Africans 'was only a prelude to their (the Basutos) extinction!' From the beginning he made it quite clear that he refused to lead a punitive expedition. All he would agree to was to go alone, or with the smallest of escorts, to meet the chiefs personally and try to work out the basis of a treaty acceptable to *both* sides. Before setting out, after very grudging approval of his proposal, he wrote a series of memoranda which included a homily on the errors of the transfer of the government of Basutoland from London to the Cape, a proposal that Basutoland should be given semi-autonomy under a Resident, a plan for a reorganization of the colonial forces, and a suggestion that he, Gordon, should be Basutoland's first Resident. These memoranda shared the fate of so many of his outpourings on paper. They remained unanswered.

Once more, as when he had bearded King Johannes, Gordon came near to losing his life after he reached the Basuto chief Masupha's kraal. The day after his arrival, Masupha's territory was attacked by a neighbouring tribe, bribed to do so by the South Africans. Masupha, convinced that Gordon had been sent as a decoy to make him think that peace was in the offing and so throw him off his guard, threatened to kill him. Again it was Gordon's indifference to the possibility of facing death that saved him. Finally Gordon's eloquence, and his frank assurance that he was on the Basutos' side, persuaded the chief to resume talks. Between them they worked out a plan to restore peace along the frontier. Back in the Cape the plan was considered totally unacceptable. Government officials would not even discuss it. Gordon reacted in his usual manner; a formal offer of resignation which, unlike the peace plan, was accepted with alacrity, the Cape Prime Minister writing — 'After your intimation that you would not fight the Basutos, and considering the tenor of your communication with Masupha, I regret to record my conviction that your continuance in the post you occupy could not be to the public interest. . .'

After less than five months Gordon left South Africa in October 1882.

His failure to work with the Cape Government, his increasing reputation of being not only a man with whom it was impossible to collaborate, but a violent eccentric with views of a near-revolutionary tendency, made it all the more unlikely that, despite promotion, he would ever be offered a job befitting his rank. The War Office was not at all anxious to have him back in England. No objection was raised, therefore, when he applied for another protracted spell of leave in order to explore the Holy Land.

For the few weeks he was in England before leaving for Palestine, he was sharply aware that he was no longer a national hero. His championing of the cause of the 'blacks' was not popular either in Whitehall or Fleet Street. Though he had always been so keen on avoiding publicity, in a queer contradictory way being ignored wounded him. The only sop to his pride was a second note from the King of the Belgians informing him that employment in the Congo was always waiting should he care to accept — 'You can name your own terms' Leopold stated, 'You know the consideration I have for your great qualities, and you cannot doubt the extreme pleasure I should always have in bearing

witness to it . . . I shall be delighted to receive verbally or in
writing a favourable answer.'

Though very much tempted, Gordon was by now so set
on his visit to the Holy Land that he turned down the offer,
saying as an excuse that he doubted whether the War Office
would release him for full time service with a foreign power.

Disembarking at Jaffa, he continued straight on to
Jerusalem with the determination to forget all about the
world and its problems, and concentrate on his exploration
of what he called the 'sources of human faith, Christian,
Jewish, Moslem.' In Jerusalem he imposed the most spartan
diet on himself, eating nothing but bread and fruit. He was
even able to give up smoking. His only relaxation was a constant
stream of letters to Augusta and Mr. Barnes. 'I do not
care for news now' he said 'I am virtually dead to what goes
on. . .'

Although the reason for his journey was, he insisted,
spiritual, there was always something of the Engineer in his
make up. It was ingrained. He became carried away by the
study of ancient sites, soon convinced that most of them
were wrongly recorded: Calvary, the Holy Sepulchre, the
Tabernacle. He claimed to have discovered the passage of the
Ark and the exact trace of the walls of old Jerusalem. When
writing in the minutest detail of his discoveries and
deductions, he also included plans of his own for a vast
project; the cutting of a canal to link the Mediterranean port
of Haifa with Akaba on the Red Sea. This project had been
inspired by a vision, strange mixture of the practical and the
ideal — 'to keep predatory Russians from Palestine and, more
important, enable all men who seek the Godly life to colonise
a well-watered and prosperous country. . .'

After several months based on Jerusalem, Gordon moved
back to the coast to Haifa, as the guest of another friend of
long standing, Laurence Oliphant, owner of a house at the
foot of Mount Carmel. It was there that he heard that Egypt
was again trouble-torn, and experienced a twinge of nostalgia

for the world he claimed to have put on one side. In frequent moments of exasperation he fulminated against Egypt and the Egyptians, but it was a form of love-hate. There was always the certitude at the back of his mind that he was the only person who understood the country's many problems and was capable of solving them. He confided to Mr. Barnes 'I do feel with my heart and soul there is work for me to perform in Egypt, but the government would never consent to employ me . . . the Khedive does not like me. . .' In the middle of one of his 'doles' brought on by these reflections, came yet another telegram from Leopold begging him to go to the Congo. He had been inactive long enough. A telegram was sent to the War Office which brought the answer 'The Secretary of State has decided to sangdon (sic) your employment in the Congo.'

Delighted at the thought that there was someone who both understood and trusted him, Gordon left Palestine in December, arriving in Brussels on New Years Day 1884. Leopold was among the very few men able to charm Gordon and break down the veneer of aloof indifference behind which he liked to shelter. He told Gordon with a disarming frankness that there was no one else capable of smashing the slavers' centuries-old hold on Central Africa. His confidence was so infectious that, on the spot, Gordon was persuaded that this must be the supreme task for which the Almighty had preserved him from death on so many battlefields. He was indeed so completely carried away by the prospect that he was hoping to leave within a day or two, when another message from London was brought to him.

The cable he had received in Haifa from the War Office had been wrongly transcribed by the clerk in the telegraph office.* It should have read that the War Office did *not* sanction either his employment (by Belgium) or his resignation. The message was accompanied by a warning that

*The telegrams actual words were '. .declines to sanction. .' instead of '. .decides to sangdon. .'

should he persist with his resignation, his pension would be forfeit.

Leopold was as upset by this astonishing communication as was Gordon, but offered to pay a cash down sum of £7,288 in compensation of loss of pension. Gordon, however, who was not only shattered but furiously angry, made up his mind to return to England, to confirm his resignation in person, and as far as possible put his domestic affairs in order. Before leaving Brussels on 6 January, he gave Leopold his solemn promise that nothing would make him change his mind and that he would be back as quickly as possible 'en route for the Congo.'

He was so impatient to be finished that he could not even wait to get to London. From Southampton he despatched his reply to the message which had upset his cherished plans — 'I have therefore' he ended 'the honour to request you to forward to His Royal Highness the Field Marshal Commander-in-Chief for the gracious approval of Her Majesty the Queen, this my humble petition to retire from Her Majesty's service. I quite understand by the warrant quoted by you that should Her Majesty graciously accept my resignation, I have no claim whatsoever for pension from Her Majesty's Government. . .'

He was sure in his own mind that the British Government was acting in a dog-in-the-manger way as far as he was concerned, and in spite of his show of outward indifference, was deeply hurt, anxious to get out of the country as quickly as possible, and with the firm intention that once the White Cliffs of Dover had faded from view, he would never again set eyes on the British Isles.

He could scarcely believe it when gradually it dawned on him that the principal reason for declining his resignation, was the realisation in official circles that he might be, after all, the only man capable of sorting out the chaotic situation existing in both Egypt and the Sudan.

7

Return to Khartoum

The situation in Egypt had degenerated to such an extent that it was a matter of major international concern, in which Britain's interest had doubled since the opening of the Suez Canal.

Ismail's extravagance and ineptitude, as has been seen, had brought Egypt to a state of bankruptcy, obliging him to accept foreign advisers, and entrust the running of the country very largely to European hands. When he tried to shake off this partial domination, the pressure of European bankers, backed by their respective governments, had forced his abdication in favour of his son Tewfik. The young Khedive had neither the experience nor the influence to save the situation. The financial position remained calamitous. The whole country was a bubbling volcano of discontent threatening to erupt at any moment.

The first grumblings came from the army, flaring into open revolt in January 1881, and was led by a peasant-born colonel, Arabi Pasha — a foretaste of the rise to power seventy years later of another peasant-born colonel, Nasser. In view of the prevalent abuses, Arabi's demands were surprisingly moderate. As spokesman for the army in general, he insisted that in future promotion should be on merit only rather than on influence and bribery of those in the right places, and that the War Minister, Osman Rifki, should be dismissed. Tewfik tried to take a strong line. He refused to parley. Arabi and his henchmen were arrested, whereupon the regiments of the Cairo garrison marched on the Abdin Palace, threatening to raze it to the ground if the prisoners were not released. Obliged to give in, Tewfik agreed to the setting up of a court of enquiry into current abuses and replaced Rifki by a pro-army politician, Mahmoud Sami.

With a little mutual trust matters might have improved, but this was totally lacking. Both Tewfik and Arabi looked on the clash which had opposed them as the first round only. After a number of minor disputes, the Khedive replaced Mahmoud with his own brother-in-law. This move, Arabi claimed, was a breach of faith. At the head of a mixed force of infantry and cavalry, backed by a battery of artillery, he staged a march on the Abdin Palace. Tewfik showed a degree of personal courage worthy of Gordon. Alone he walked up to the mutineers and ordered them to disperse. Arabi, arguing from strength, was not impressed. He would only march his men away, he said, on being given the assurance that the government would be completely reorganized. Once more Tewfik was obliged to give in. Mahmoud Sami was re-instated in the War Ministry. From that moment, Egyptian nationalism, as represented by Arabi, became the dominant political factor in the country.

By now sure of his own power, Arabi started to stir up anti-foreign feelings by organizing riots and demonstrations, the battle cry being that 'Egyptians were imprisoned, exiled, strangled, thrown into the Nile according to the will of their (foreign) masters. A liberated slave was a freer man than a free-born Arab. . .'

Powerless to halt the movement, Tewfik tried to muzzle it by inviting Arabi to enter the government as Under Secretary for War, while Britain and France, increasingly alarmed by the growing chauvinistic trend, ordered their diplomatic representatives to present the Khedive with a jointly signed note declaring that the two European powers would support to the hilt his tenure of the throne, and that anybody who might seek to overthrow the established order, would find 'Britain and France united to oppose them. . .'

It was a tactless — and calamitous — move. Rather than strengthening Tewfik's position, it served as a propaganda handle for Arabi's accusations that the Khedive was nothing but the foreigners' lacquey, unable to make any decision without first seeking the approval of his European masters. In an attempt to appease the nationalists Tewfik dissolved the government and set up a new administration with Mahmoud Sami as Prime Minister and Arabi, minister of War.

This latest success went to Arabi's head. Instant dismissal of all foreigners in Egyptian service was demanded, while Osman Rifki together with fifty ex-government officials were arrested, tried *in camera*, and condemned to be deported to the Sudan. In desperation Tewfik commuted the sentences. Mahmoud Sami resigned, and Tewfik then found himself in the humiliating position of not being able to find a single politician who either would, or dared, accept nomination. Finally he was forced, much to the fury of both Britain and France, to beg Sami to go back on his resignation and re-assume office.

The late 19th century, however, was still the era of 'gunboat' politics.

A joint Anglo-French naval squadron was despatched to cruise off the roads of Alexandria, to quell the fears of the city's large European population and as a reminder to the Egyptians of allied armed strength. Again the move proved a bad psychological error. Violence in the form of anti-European riots broke out all over the country, stirred up by

Arabi's agitators. In the first few days over fifty died as a result of mob fury while panic-stricken crowds besieged harbours and land frontiers. Since most of Egypt's commerce was in the hands of British, French, or Greeks, chaos reigned, worsened when fanatical Egyptian troops began to install batteries on Alexandria's sea front, ignoring warnings that if the work continued the allied fleet would open fire.

On the morning of 11 July, British ships — the French had in the meantime backed out fearing the reaction of pro-Egyptian sentiments in Algeria — began a systematic bombardment which ended in the total destruction of the Egyptian batteries, followed by the landing of a force of infantry and Royal Marines which occupied the city after a brief but fierce resistance. On his own initiative, Arabi Pasha then proclaimed that a state of 'irreconciliable war exists between the Egyptians and the English'.

Though the French were still unwilling to co-operate, the British government decided on independent action. A brigade was sent from Cyprus, bringing the strength of the British contingent to 5,000, command of the force being given to Sir Garnet Wolseley. In spite of the blistering heat, Wolseley marched rapidly on Ismailia, one of the key points of the Suez Canal, which was occupied after only token opposition, then, turning inland, met and defeated the main Egyptian army at Tel-el-Kebir. Utterly demoralized, the Egyptians were incapable of offering further resistance. Arabi himself surrendered, was sentenced to death but had the sentence commuted to life imprisonment on the island of Ceylon.

After the first satisfaction following on Arabi's disappearance from the scene, it became increasingly evident that Britain was more heavily involved than ever before in Egyptian affairs. She had become a protective power. There was a British force in the country ostensibly to ensure law and order, but which to all intents and purposes was an army of occupation. British officials were in key governmental positions. Arabi's nationalist outburst had still further worsened the financial outlook, and now to add to the embarrassment of this forced adoption of a hesitant imperial role, both Turkey and France were angered by Britain's monopoly in such a vital strategic area.

But as the liberal Prime Minister Gladstone was pondering the best way to extricate himself from the Egyptian tangle, a threat to Egyptian security, far more serious than the revolt of Arabi and his fellow officers, was raising its head in the Sudan.

In 1833, a carpenter of Dongola on the Nile became the father of yet another son who he called Mahomet Ahmed. Though the carpenter claimed to be a descendant of the Prophet Mohammed himself, he was a poor man and happy to be able to apprentice the young Mahomet Ahmed to his uncle, a boat-builder, when he reached the age of twelve.

The apprentice found the work uncongenial. It was not that he was lazy. But he was observant and quick witted. Building boats was heavy work and we are told that the boy 'could think of no good reason why he should slave all day for next to nothing when he saw *fakirs* living on the fat of the land for little more than a prayer or two and a saintly demeanour'. It cannot be denied, therefore, that this first interest in his faith was based largely on commercial interest!

However, once he had attached himself to a *fakirs'* school, he began to display an acolyte's enthusiasm, especially for the more ascetic aspects of Islamic teaching. Soon he was upbraiding his masters for their worldliness, even going as far as to create a scandal at a party given by a *fakir* to celebrate the birth of a son, calling down Allah's curses on his host's head for permitting singing and dancing, both forbidden by the Koran.

On becoming a *fakir* himself, and to prove that he was one of the elect, Mahomet Ahmed retired from everyday life to an island on the Nile where he made his home in a cistern. It was said that during the six years he lived there, from 1874 to 1880, shut off from the world, he spent most of his time repeating outloud the many qualifications attached to the name of Allah, and surrounding himself with clouds of incense. There were frequent visitors to see this eccentric, individuals to begin with, then as his fame spread, large crowds anxious not only to see, but to hear him preach. Over the years Mahomet Ahmed had developed a fiery eloquence especially when denouncing sinners and infidels, that was able to sway a mob. It was also noticed that on the rare occasions when he smiled his centre teeth sloped outwards in the shape of a sharply outlined V. This, it was soon rumoured, was a mystic sign — 'All believed so. "Abu Fulaja" they cried in an ecstasy "Father of the V-shaped gap!"'. Adoringly they laid their gifts before him and shuffled out backwards. . .'

It may seem surprising that Mahomet Ahmed, holy man and noted castigator of luxury and advocate of poverty's purifying qualities, was prepared to accept presents. But there was a streak of the material blended with the ascetic in his nature, as well as a craving for worldly power to bolster the spiritual domination he was able to exercise.

In 1880, when the disillusioned Gordon was leaving the Sudan after resigning his post of Governor-General, Mahomet Ahmed had convinced himself that he was at the very least a prophet. A year later he proclaimed that it had been revealed to him in visions that he was the successor of the Prophet Mahommed himself, 'The Mahdi', whose coming 'in the fullness of time' had been foretold centuries earlier.

As soon as he had persuaded not only himself but tens of thousands of his fellow Sudanese that there could be no possible doubt that he was indeed the Mahdi, the great reformer, the instrument of Allah who would gather the whole world into Islam's fold — voluntarily or by force — he had no hesitation in declaring the *Jihad* or Holy War. Nevertheless it was not an infidel, but a fellow Moslem community that was the first to feel the Mahdi's damaging power.

Though he had no idea of the art of warfare, the fanatical horde of his followers made up in reckless courage and indifference to death what they lacked in military skills. The first trial of strength came with Bashi Bazouks forming the Egyptian garrison of Khartoum.

The Sudan's Governor-General was Raouf Pasha, the man who Gordon had dismissed from his service in Equatoria for corruption, a man who had remained not only corrupt but totally inefficient and who owed his high position to bribery and treachery. Alarmed at rumours of trouble in outlying districts, Raouf sent a messenger to the man who was calling himself the Mahdi to order him to proceed to Khartoum immediately and give himself up as a prisoner if he and his followers wished to have their lives spared. The reply was far from reassuring — 'Tell your master' said the Mahdi 'that if his soldiers fire on me and my followers, their bullets will not hurt me or them and if you advance against us with steamers they will sink with everyone on board. . .'

Raouf accepted the challenge. An expeditionary force was sent to deal with the madman. It was totally defeated. Hardly a man survived, and the Mahdi, quick to take advantage of this first major victory, over-ran the province of Kardofan, setting up a temporary capital at Jebel Gedir in accordance with an old legend that when the true Mahdi did appear it would be on the slopes of Jebel Moussa. This latter mountain is in fact the African Pillar of Hercules and faces Gibraltar, but mere geography did not discourage the Mahdi. All maps he stated flatly were mistaken. *This* was the real Jebel Moussa, he declared in a re-naming ceremony. The Sudanese were more than prepared to believe him. What was a mere map compared with the word of Allah's representative on earth? They came flocking in ever increasing numbers to rally to his banners.

A second expedition sent — but not led — by Raouf, 1,500 strong, like the first was slaughtered to a man, and a few months later a third, this time at least 6,000, met the same fate. Having disposed of Raouf's Bashi-Bazouks, the Mahdi then marched on El Obeid, Kardofan's official capital. The city's high walls proved a temporary barrier, but the inhabitants had no stomach for a long siege, and the gates were opened in January 1883.

This last success dispelled any doubts that might have existed in the minds of the majority of the Sudanese as to Mahomet Ahmed's claim to be the true Mahdi. Fanaticism for his cause swept the entire province so that once the fall of El Obeid became known, he found himself at the head of an army of at least 100,000 who had shown on the battlefield that brave men with no fear of death, armed only with sword or spear, were more than a match for armies equipped with modern rifles, but with no heart for the fight.

The Cairo government at last became aware of the menace from the south. The next army sent against the Mahdi was placed under the command of an Englishman, Colonel William Hicks, better known as Hicks Pasha. In the meantime the Mahdi had taken over Darfur and his influence spread from the Nile to the Red Sea. When many of the slavers threw in their lot with him, his wild host of spearman was backed up by small groups of well-armed mercenaries who had formed the nucleus of the slave chiefs' private armies. Some sort of discipline and organization was also being instilled into the Mahdi's masses who were learning to fight in formation and manoeuvre to a leader's commands rather than on the principle of each man for himself. Great stress was laid on the stern observance of religious laws. One is rather reminded of the Tien Wang's 'model' army. Moral lapses were punished by the *Kourbash*, a heavy whip; one hundred lashes for smoking, eighty for drinking alcohol. It was also stressed by the Mahdi (although himself a wealthy man) that poverty was a supreme virtue, and on this principle was based the Dervish — as his followers were usually known — uniform; the *jibbeh,* a rough white smock covered with black and brown patches.

On paper, Hicks Pasha's army should have been capable of dealing with Mahdism. Very well armed with modern rifles and the latest model field guns, it totalled just over ten thousand, but its manoeuvrability was hopelessly impaired by a baggage train of 6,000 camels and a horde of camp followers. Nor did the fact that Hicks himself spent most of his time quarrelling with his immediate subordinates help to weld his army into a cohesive fighting force.

Organization was lamentable. Rations were short. Progress was held up when it was found that many of the wells en route had been filled in. Many of the guides through the practically uncharted country were Mahdi sympathisers.

The march had lasted over two months when, on 1 November when nearing El Obeid the column was attacked by 50,000 Dervishes. It was a massacre. Hicks himself was killed and of the total force which had set out, a bare 250 survived. In addition twenty guns, thousands of rifles and tens of thousands of rounds of ammunition fell into the Mahdi's hands. It was the hour of his greatest triumph. On hearing of the extermination of the Hicks column, every Egyptian garrison, with the exception of Khartoum and some of the more important Nile stations, surrendered. The situation was summed up in an article in the English press, — 'the days of Egypt's dominion in the Sudan are now numbered. Mahdism is marching to victory and there is nothing that anyone can do to stop it. . .'

Gordon was surprised when the very evening he reached England, the editor of the influential daily paper, the *Pall Mall Gazette,* called on him personally to find out his views on the Sudan question, and still more so when in the course of their talks he learned that the British government was advising Tewfik to cut his losses and abandon the whole of the Sudan to the Mahdi. His astonishment soon turned to anger. Such a solution, he told the editor, Mr. W.T.Stead, indignantly, was highly dishonourable, adding forcibly that there would never have been a Mahdi if only the Khedive had listened to his, Gordon's, advice. The Mahdi was nothing more than a charlatan, created by Egyptian corruption and misrule. With a proper Sudanese government presided over by a just Governor-General who had the people's interests at heart, the Mahdi would soon collapse. But there could be no half measures such as a temporary withdrawal of Cairo's authority — 'You must either surrender absolutely to the Mahdi or defend Khartoum at all hazards' he insisted.

Next day the *Gazette's* headline was CHINESE GORDON FOR THE SUDAN. Though Stead did not know it at the time, his paper was echoing opinions already voiced in government circles. Lord Granville, Foreign Secretary, had received a letter saying 'There is one man who is competent to deal with the question; Charlie Gordon. . .', while from Cairo, Sir Evelyn Baring, who had clashed so frequently with Gordon in the past, was suggesting, with Gordon at the back of his mind, that 'a capable British officer should be sent out immediately in order to ensure an orderly withdrawal.'

The *Gazette's* article was the first of many in the London press, which seemed suddenly to remember that Gordon, who a few years ago had been so conveniently forgotten, was indeed genius and hero, the only man to straighten out the Sudan mess. Unable to pick up a newspaper without seeing his name mentioned, Gordon was not altogether surprised when on 12 January he received a telegram from Lord Wolseley asking him to call at the War Office. When the two old friends met, Wolseley told Gordon that whatever promises he might have made to the Belgian king, before he could accept employment in the Congo there was an urgent task for him to undertake in the service of his own country. At the same time Lord Granville was pressing Baring to persuade Tewfik, who remembered with considerable rancour the way Gordon had spoken about him, to forget the past and agree to the temporary re-employment of the Sudan's ex-Governor General.

It was a very difficult and embarrassing situation for Gordon. His promise to Leopold had been formal. He had sworn not once but many times that Egypt had seen the last of him, and had also made it very clear that he was in complete disagreement with the policy of evacuation. Yet all the time he was obsessed with the conviction that no one else held the key to the situation, and though he knew that the orders he would be given would of a necessity run contrary to his beliefs, he accepted without argument, or, as far as is known, any attempt to put across his own views. That same evening he was writing to Augusta to the effect that his appointment to the Congo might have to be put off for a couple of months as he would first be going to make a report on the situation in the Sudan.

For the sake of politeness, he felt duty bound to pay a brief visit to Brussels to let the King know of his decision. Leopold was disappointed — Gordon actually reported that he was 'furious' — and their farewell, which took place the next day, Gordon having remained a bare twenty-four hours in Belgium, was frosty; perhaps understandably.

By the time he was back in London, the news of 'Chinese Gordon's' appointment was official, the *Times* commenting 'It is impossible to exaggerate the feelings of relief and satisfaction universally inspired by the knowledge that General Gordon has undertaken the pacification of the Sudan. . .'

There had, however, been many objections behind the scenes. Baring had had second thoughts about Gordon's reappearance on the Egyptian scene 'He (Gordon) must fully understand that he must take his instructions from the British representative in Egypt and report to him' he had written. Gladstone, who had never liked Gordon, describing him as a 'dangerous fellow with a bee in his bonnet', was only won over by the Foreign Secretary on being assured that it was after all only a rescue mission, and not an imperialist adventure that was contemplated.

The actual departure took place on January 18. It was a haphazard affair. At the last moment Gordon had let it be known that he had no money. While he was dining, Wolseley did a round of the London clubs and collected £300 in gold. The Duke of Cambridge and Lord Granville, who had bought the tickets, were at Charing Cross station where they were joined by Lord Wolseley accompanied by Gordon's nephew, the latter carrying a metal suitcase containing his uncle's uniforms.

When at last Gordon arrived with Colonel D.H.Stewart of the 11th Hussars who was to act as his deputy, it was the Duke of Cambridge who held the carriage door open for him, while Wolseley who had once said that he was 'not fit to pipeclay his (Gordon's) belt' and that he was 'one of the few friends I have ever had who came up to my estimate of the Christian hero', gave him his gold watch and chain and all the spare cash in his pocket.

The calmest man present was Gordon himself. Later while travelling by train — being a bad sailor, he was making as much of the journey as possible overland — he wrote to Augusta 'I am not a bit moved and hope to do the people good. Lord Granville said Ministers were very much obliged to me. I said I was honoured. I telegraphed the King of the Belgians and told him "Wait a few months". Kindest love to all — your affectionate brother C.G. Gordon.'

His instructions were perfectly clear. They stated:- 'Her Majesty's Government are desirous that you should proceed at once to Suakin to report to them on the military situation in the Sudan, and on the measures which it may be advisable to take for the security of the Egyptian garrisons still holding positions in that country, and for the safety of the European population in Khartoum.

'You are also desired to consider and report upon the best method of evacuation of the interior of the Sudan, and the manner in which the safety and good administration by the Egyptian government of the ports of the Red Sea coast can best be secured.

'In connection with this subject you should pay especial consideration to the question of the steps that may usefully be taken to counteract the stimulus which it is feared may possibly be given to the slave trade by the present insurrectionary movement and by the withdrawal of Egyptian authority from the interior.

'You will be under the instructions of Her Majesty's Agent and Consul General at Cairo, through whom your reports to Her Majesty's Government should be sent under flying seal.

'You will consider yourself authorized and instructed to perform such duties as the Egyptian Government may care to entrust to you and may be communicated to you by Sir Evelyn Baring. You will be accompanied by Colonel Stewart who will assist you in the duties confided to you.

'On your arrival in Egypt, you will at once communicate with Sir Evelyn Baring who will arrange to meet you and will settle with you whether you should proceed direct to Suakin, or should go yourself or despatch Colonel Stewart to Khartoum via the Nile.'

These instructions would seem absolutely clear, and the fact that Gordon had agreed to undertake the mission, to indicate that he had no objections to make concerning the government's evacuation policy. Yet from the very beginning misunderstandings arose, followed by disputes, contradictions, orders and counter orders.

The old slaver Zubehr was the subject of the first of these wrangles which flared up a couple of days after Gordon's arrival in Cairo. During the voyage Gordon claimed that he had had a mystic revelation. The whole Sudan problem could be solved if Zubehr were to be released from his state of 'open arrest' and be nominated Governor-General of the Sudan with Gordon as his adviser to put him on the right track. Baring agreed that the 'Black Khedive' might be the only man who could dare to oppose the Mahdi with any hope of success, but was unwilling to consider employing a notorious slaver, nor could he understand how Gordon could even suggest an alliance with a man he had spent years fighting, whom he had frequently described as one of the world's greatest scoundrels, and who never sought to disguise the fact that he was determined to avenge the death of his son, Suliman, whose execution, he stressed, was plain murder. However, Gordon was so adamant, and became so excited at being opposed, that Baring agreed to arrange a private interview, insisting that he too should be present while it took place.

The confrontation was dramatic. Zubehr listened to Gordon's generalities in silence, but when with that strange tactlessness so typical of him, he mentioned Suliman's death, he accused him of being an assassin. Gordon could perhaps, in view of the circumstances, have argued that the actual execution order was given by Gessi and that at the time he, Gordon, had been many hundreds of miles away. Instead he argued that Suliman had been a rebel who had richly deserved his fate. This was too much for the Black Khedive. He got to his feet to signify that the interview was ended, and as Gordon left shouted 'The blood feud is between us. . .'

The meeting with Tewfik was cordial, though limited to an exchange of formalities and inquiries as to the other's state of health. Serious discussions were held in the British representative's office with only Sir Evelyn Wood and the elderly Nubar Pasha, now once more Prime Minister, present as final plans were drawn up by Gordon and Baring. From the beginning Baring made the official position quite clear. He agreed that too rapid a withdrawal might give the impression that the Khedive admitted that the Mahdi was too strong for him and thus diminish hopes of a future re-occupation, but stressed the fact time and again that *temporary* evacuation of the Sudan was inevitable and the official government policy. So that there should be no mistake, after Gordon had been appointed Governor-General for the second time, Baring had another set of instructions drawn up, a long document which included the important phrase — 'You are therefore given full discretion to retain the troops for such reasonable period as you may think necessary in order that the abandonment of the country may be accomplished with the least possible risk to life and property. . .'

For his part Gordon gave Baring to understand that he was in complete agreement with this policy of 'evacuation', and with another important decision reached; that once the Mahdi had been crushed, autonomy would be granted to the old Sultanate families of the provinces.

When Gordon and Colonel Stewart left Cairo on January 26, Gordon was depressed by his failure to win over Zubehr. The slow journey gave him too much time to think, with the result that he came to certain basic, but erroneous, conclusions which were to prove fatal.

Although in Cairo he had been warned that the Mahdi was a truly formidable power exercising an hypnotic influence over his followers, a streak of Victorian snobbery, combined with a tendency to wishful thinking, made him under-estimate his enemy. He had, he kept telling Colonel Stewart, triumphed over infinitely more formidable opponents — notably the Tien Wang — in the past. And if he could crush the Taipings, then he could certainly crush an upstart of *humble origin* like the Mahdi and expose him as the fake he undoubtedly was. In fact the more he thought the matter over, the more convinced he became that Mahdism was an easily prickable bubble and, this being the case, the *policy of evacuation was a grave mistake.*

Once again Gordon had changed his mind, a mind now seething with new ideas for the ultimate solution which he hurried to note down on paper. In his new-found enthusiasm, he wrote to Leopold saying he did not expect to be long in the Sudan and was much looking forward to taking up his duties in the Congo. Bad news had no effect, even when he heard that Samuel Baker's brother Valentine, in command of a column marching to relieve Egyptian Red Sea coast garrisons had had it cut to pieces, a defeat which meant that one of the only two escape routes from Khartoum, that to the port of Suakin, was blocked. He laughed when he was given a frantic message from Gladstone himself suggesting that in view of the disaster he might like to abandon the mission altogether, replying that in his opinion he had every chance of success, for, he ended 'In spite of all, I believe that God will bless our efforts.' He was not even perturbed when handed a report that the Mahdi's forces had swelled to the astronomical figure of 300,000, and would soon be in a position to stop all river traffic down the Nile. 'I hope' he wrote to Mr. Barnes, 'that in a month, D.V., the country will be quiet and the roads open. . .'

Before reaching Khartoum, he stopped at Berber to meet local chiefs after sending a telegram to be read aloud by criers to the people of the capital —'Do not be panic stricken. Ye are men, not women. I am coming. Gordon.'

Berber, just above the 5th cataract, was a key strategic point on the Nile, so much so that Khartoum's existence depended largely on the loyalty of its inhabitants. This he was determined to ensure, but in his meeting with the chiefs was guilty of a grave psychological error.

The Sheiks were well aware of the importance of their decision, which they viewed from a strictly materialistic point of view. They wished to be on the winning side and were inclined to think that the Khedive would triumph in the end, basing this surmise on the fact that if the great Gordon Pasha were with them, it meant that the British army which had smashed Arabi Pasha with such ease would be marching against the Mahdi. Their astonishment and dismay can be imagined when they learnt of Egypt's intention to evacuate the Sudan. Gordon had imagined that they would be

111

delighted at the prospect of autonomy and the possibility of continuing the profitable 'black ivory' trade without interference. His judgment was completely at fault. The Sheiks saw plainly that any territory given up by the Khedive would immediately be seized by the Mahdi. 'With protests of devotion they dispersed across the desert for the most part convinced that the sooner they were under the Mahdi's protection the better, for the Mahdi was in the habit of confiscating all the worldly goods of those who were slow to acknowledge him. . .'

This lapse on Gordon's part is all the more extraordinary in that, as has been seen, he had already come to the conclusion that evacuation would not be necessary. Nor, despite his experience of the country and its people, had he taken into account the fact that deep in the heart of even the most venal of slavers, the spark of religious fanaticism lay dormant.

Satisfied that both by his diplomacy and his personality he had assured the safe tenure of Berber, he was in the highest of spirits as he continued up river. He was indeed so pleased with himself that, without consulting Baring or any other authority either in London or Cairo, he wrote to the Mahdi, a friendly but paternal letter, in which after stressing his own supreme authority as the Sudan's Governor-General he offered him the Sultanate of Kordofan — accompanying the offer with richly decorated Sultan's robes — provided he would promise to behave himself in the future and immediately cease from all revolutionary activities.

The Mahdi's reply was devastatingly logical. As Kardofan was already in his hands, he pointed out that 'he had no need to accept a gift from someone who no longer possessed what he purported to offer.' Gordon's momentary good humour was proof against the snub. He still thought of the Mahdi as a recalcitrant youngster whose 'difficult' behaviour amused him in much the same way that that of a mischievous, but high-spirited, pupil might amuse an understanding master.

And when he heard that the Mahdi's forces were on the move towards Khartoum, he sent a postcard to Mr. Barnes — 'I do not believe in the advance of the Mahdi. I am very hopeful for mens' hearts are in His hands. . .'

If Gordon had over-estimated his personal influence on the Berber Sheiks, he was surprised by the near hysteria of the rapturous welcome he received on his entry into Khartoum on the 18th February.

The Sudanese capital had, for some months, been living under the shadow of mortal fear, expecting any moment to see the patched-smock-uniformed Dervish army swarming round the city walls. Nobody had the slightest confidence in the ability of the Egyptian garrison to hold out let alone its commander, Colonel de Coetlogon, who had never stopped bombarding Cairo with telegrams urging immediate withdrawal. Frank Power the *Times* correspondent echoed the Colonel's views. He stated categorically that the city housed a huge 'fifth column', as it would be called these days, only waiting for the attack from outside to dig up carefully hidden arms caches, open the gates, and join in the massacre of all those who had the temerity to resist the authority of Allah's representative on earth. But Power's flagging spirits revived when he heard that 'Chinese Gordon' was on the way. 'They could not have sent a better man' he wrote enthusiastically 'I don't believe the fellows in Lucknow looked more anxiously for Colin Campbell than we look for Gordon.'

He had judged public opinion nicely.

As soon as Gordon appeared, he was mobbed by the crowd. He was their deliverer. There could have been no greater contrast with his first entry when the people kept sulkily off the streets. He was called the Father Protector. Men and women grovelled to try to kiss his feet; children were pushed towards him so that they would be blessed by mere contact with his body. But their hysterical joy was short lived. For the second time in a few days, Gordon totally misjudged popular sentiment. His welcome had been delirious because everybody firmly believed that he would be arriving at the head, or just ahead, of a powerful army which would include a hard core of British regulars.

They were shattered, therefore, when from the Palace Gordon delivered another of those brief addresses for which he was famous — 'I come without soldiers, but with God on my side, to redress the wrongs of the Sudan. I will not fight with soldiers, but with justice. . .'

Without soldiers! The people of Khartoum could scarcely believe their ears. From the heights of optimism public morale dropped to the lowest depths. The Governor-General must be mad — a dangerous madman who could only lessen their already slender chances of survival. It made no difference when Gordon started putting his promise of justice into practice by burning tax registers and tax collectors' whips in the street, pulling down gaols, and striking the chains from prisoners' hands and feet. Though bringing some comfort to the poor and the persecuted, they did nothing to dispel the fear weighing down rich and poor alike. Without soldiers what could Gordon do to protect them from the Mahdi? Gordon said that God was on his side. The Mahdi proclaimed not only that Allah was on *his* side, but that he was the chosen of Allah and that all who opposed his will would be destroyed, and while Gordon was a lone figure, the Mahdi had more than quarter of a million fanatical soldiers to make sure his edicts were obeyed.

Power was suffering from acute hero-worship. He was sending back optimistic reports to the *Times* and writing excitedly to his friends that 'no one could do other than like such a lovable character' going as far as to assert 'he (Gordon) is indeed, I believe, the greatest and best man of the century'. Yet within a week, ten days at the most, Gordon himself realised that he had failed, that his speech had been a possibly fatal mistake. The once magic words 'Gordon Pasha' could no longer bring mighty and lowly alike flocking to his spiritual standard. For the people of the Sudan the word of Allah now carried more weight than the word of God.

There was still cheering when he appeared in the streets, even a few isolated incidents of attempted foot kissing. But not one of the local Sheiks had come to pay his respects, and after that unfortunate announcement that he had come 'without soldiers' those who had most benefited by his spectacular reforms were already asking themselves on whose side their vital interests lay. Trying to revoke the impression that he was dictating from weakness, a number of small mobile columns were sent out to try to persuade the recalcitrant Sheiks to come to Khartoum for talks. They simply vanished beyond the vast horizons. Some of the columns were fired on, while from outlying districts came news of Dervish bands moving as if to cut communications with Berber.

Reacting angrily, Gordon tried to switch to strong arm methods. A second proclamation was made — 'Since my arrival here, I have constantly advised you to the effect that good treatment and justice would be accorded to the natives and that they should desist from rebellion which only leads to war and bloodshed. Finding however that this advice had no effect on some of the people, I have been compelled to have recourse to severe measures, contrary to my own inclinations, so much so that the troops of the British Government are now on their way and in a few days will be in Khartoum. Whoever persists in wicked conduct will then have the treatment he deserves.'

This statement was yet another, probably the greatest, of Gordon's errors in the handling of the Sudan question. He was perfectly well aware that it was the British Government's unbending policy not to become seriously involved with the Mahdi. He had been told categorically in England, and again by Baring in Cairo, that under no circumstances whatsoever could he expect reinforcements. It is true that when this proclamation was issued British and Indian troops, under the command of Sir Gerald Graham V.C., numbering about 4,000, were at Suakin to deny the Red Sea ports to the Mahdi's ally, Osman Digna. But again he knew their role was purely defensive, and that any question of a march from the coast to help Khartoum was ruled out.

It may be that because so often in the past by dogged perseverance he had managed to get policies reversed, Gordon could not believe that if the worst came to the worst, the British Government would stand aside as spectators while he himself, his garrison, and all those citizens of Khartoum loyal to the Khedive, fell to the Dervishes' spears and double-edged crusader swords. But even if he had had this conviction, he must have known the risk he was running by setting down in black and white what was, after all, a deliberate falsehood concerning the arrival of 'troops of the British Government', and qualifying news of this purely fictitious arrival with the remark 'in a few days will be in Khartoum. . .' And the inevitable happened.

When the proclamation was heard there was a tremendous resurgence of morale, but as the days slipped past and no promised troops appeared either down the desert tracks or on river steamers, depression set in, aggravated by the suspicion that Gordon Pasha, whose word till then had been his bond, had deliberately broadcast false information.

In the meantime Gordon was making every effort to ratify his promise by sending a copy of the proclamation to Baring and bombarding him with telegrams. Baring was appalled. He could do nothing but send the telegrams back to London as soon as they arrived, and his troubles were increased when Gordon suddenly returned to the attack about the necessity of re-instating Zubehr.

The few replies London could be bothered to send off were, of course, negative, and their effect was to bring out yet another of those strange contradictions abounding in Gordon's character. He dug his toes in. Though paying lip service to the continued orders to withdraw, he had already made up his mind to hang on, and that in any case he himself would never leave the city, a determination based again on the ever present death wish. 'I feel so very much inclined to wish it' he wrote to Augusta 'His will might be my release. Earth's joys grow very dim.'

At the same time he longed to 'save the Sudan' urging that if the country were abandoned it would only increase the Mahdi's lust for conquest. 'If Egypt is to be quiet, the Mahdi must be smashed up. . .I repeat that evacuation is possible, but you will feel the effect in Egypt and will be forced to enter into a far more serious affair in order to guard Egypt. . '

This constant pressure did react on Baring. He began to wonder whether Gordon were not right after all, whether for the sake of both Egypt and the Sudan it would not be better to hang on in the hope that the Mahdi's prestige might be undermined or, as Gordon put it, he might be 'smashed up...' He was encouraged in this latter hope by the fact that twice within three weeks, Sir Gerald Graham's British and Indian regulars, had inflicted severe defeats on Osman Digna's Dervishes, so ending the Mahdi's reputation of invincibility. This, however, made no difference to London. Orders and objectives remained the same, while the suggestion that the old slaver Zubehr should receive a British decoration and become Governor General of the Sudan raised a storm of protests and questions as to Gordon's sanity. But Gordon was quite unperturbed; each formal rejection was followed by another demand. Finally he made yet another mistake to add to the chaplet of errors which had marked his behaviour since setting foot on Egyptian soil. He sent for Frank Power, *Times* correspondent, persuading him to send back an article — probably with the idea of forcing Gladstone's hand — in which it was strongly hinted that the British Government had given its blessing to Zubehr's appointment.

Publication of the article created an uproar. Questions were asked in the House of Commons. Gladstone, aware that anything short of a strenuous denial could well lose him millions of votes, publicly announced his disapproval. At the same time Lord Glanville, acting on the Prime Minister's orders, wrote an angry letter to Baring hammering home the fact that Zubehr's employment could not be given any consideration whatsoever, that Khartoum could expect *no* reinforcements, and that it was high time the evacuation got under way.

After March 12, telegraphic communication became sporadic as bands of Dervishes started cutting the lines. On April 9, however, Grodon was able to send a long telegram containing what amounted to a threat; — 'You state your intention of not sending any relief force up here or to Berber and you refuse me Zubehr. I (therefore) consider myself free to act according to circumstances. I shall hold on here as long as I can and if I can suppress the rebellion I shall do so. If I cannot I shall retire to the Equator and leave you the indelible disgrace of abandoning the garrisons. of Sennar, Kassala, Berber and Dongola, with the certainty that you will eventually be forced to smash up the Mahdi under great difficulties, if you would retain peace in Egypt.'

He knew when he sent this message that there was now no hope of those mythical 'troops of the British Government' whose speedy arrival he had announced so glibly. He should have realised at the same time that he had no chance whatsoever of being able to 'suppress the rebellion' and this being the case there was only one path left open; to obey orders and start organizing the evacuation without a further moment's delay. He still had the means at his disposal, including a flotilla of ten river steamers. Till May Berber was still firmly in the hands of those loyal to the Khedive. Khartoum could have been cleared both of its garrison and foreign (including Egyptian) population, probably without the loss — other than by accident or from sickness — of a single life.

The root of the trouble was that Gordon could not, or

would not, admit that a 'low born' person like the Mahdi could actually wield more influence than Gordon Pasha. Even at this stage he was still talking of Mahdism as 'trumpery', and could still write, apparently sincerely, 'if you would get by good pay 3,000 Turkish infantry and 1,000 Turkish cavalry, the affair, including the crushing of the Mahdi, would be accomplished in four months. .' And he added with spite, not quite in keeping with his character 'After the way these people have rejected my terms, I would be inclined to let the Turkish harrow go over them. . .'

It was a major tragedy that because of this stubborn obstinacy, thousands of men, women and children, as well as Gordon himself, were to lose their lives in a struggle contrary to orders, and doomed from the very beginning.

8

The Trap

Once he had made up his mind to stay, Gordon set about reviewing the forces at his disposal, and bringing his Engineer-trained brain to bear on the problem of improving the defences.

With determined men, Khartoum would have been easy to hold. The city stands on a triangular-shaped peninsula bounded by the White Nile and the Blue Nile, the triangle's apex being the junction of the two rivers. The only land approach was the triangle's base. Gordon saw to it that this vulnerable access was well protected. Trenches were dug, reinforced by bastions at regular intervals, in turn covered by barbed wire entanglements and fields of land mines. Though the city walls were within range from either river bank, Gordon looked on his river steamers not simply as a means of escape, but as offensive weapons. Guns were mounted on their decks — he remembered his successes with the *Hyson* in his Ever Victorious Army days — their sides plated with *ad hoc* locally forged armour. With these mobile, floating

batteries, he was able to break up many a Dervish con-
centration in the early days of the siege.

When he took over, the garrison totalled roughly 8,000
infantry with an artillery element, and 3,000 Sudanese and
negro volunteers. On paper it was an impressive force, but in
Gordon's own words, 'at least one third of the (Egyptian)
troops were unreliable' Very few had any wish to fight. The
best of the lot was a group of the negroes; former slaves.
Altogether it was poor material to oppose the Mahdi's death
or glory minded Dervishes.

The city itself was not attractive. 'Seen from the Nile it
presented a view of a mass of dirty grey houses, with the
minaret of the one large mosque standing out. There was
only one street of any importance lined with dung covered
buildings from which opened the palace gardens, and in
which was to be found the arsenal, a hospital built on
Gordon's orders during his first tour as Governor-General, the
barracks, two smaller mosques and a church.' But even in this
street the stench was so appalling that most Europeans
walked along it holding camphor soaked handkerchiefs to
their noses.

The civilian population, about 50,000, presented a grave
problem. In case of a siege, how could so many mouths be fed?
As many as possible were sent down river, till by April
there were only five Europeans left; Gordon himself, Frank
Power and Colonel Stewart, Herbin the French Consul and
the Austrian consul Hansal, a man of whom Gordon
thoroughly disapproved as being too fond of good living, and
to whom he refused resolutely to address a single word.

In April, there was a moment when Gordon's optimism
might have appeared justified, though the moment was sadly
short lived.

Despite his fanaticism and firm belief in his divine
mission, the Mahdi also had a strong practical streak in his
character. He had been very badly rattled by the two defeats

inflicted on his men by Graham's regulars. Could they, he asked himself, be a sign that his temporal power had reached, if not already passed, its apogee? And if that were so, would he not be well advised to accept Gordon's offer of the Sultanate of Kardofan and come to terms, if only temporarily, with the Khedive's representative?

Some believe that a letter of acceptance was actually written but for reasons unknown never sent, but the more plausible explanation is that the Mahdi never made up his mind definitely to such an act of virtual submission, preferring to retire to meditate waiting for inspiration from Allah to dictate future policy. In this case the answer was provided not from on high, but by Sir Gerald Graham.

After Osman Digna's second defeat, the Mahdi expected that Graham would detach a column from his main force — as indeed Gordon begged him to do — march to Berber, and so secure that vital communication centre. Graham himself would have liked to have gone to the help of a comrade, but his orders were rigid. His was not an offensive role. Under no circumstances was he to undertake any operations inland. Short of taking a leaf out of Gordon's book and turning a blind eye on directives — which he was not prepared to do — he had no alternative but to fall back on Suakin.

For the Mahdi, this was a direct sign from Heaven that, in spite of his losses, Allah was still on his side. He settled down to write a long letter to Gordon, whom he was now beginning to admire as a brave man and near spiritual equal, in which he set out his own terms for the conclusion of a settlement.

'From the servant of his God, Mohammed el Mahdi ibn Es Sayid Abdulla, to the dear one of Britain and of the Khedive, Gordon Pasha.

'I am a humble servant, a lover of poverty and of the poor, one of those who hates the pride and haughtiness of those rulers whom I wish to lead in the way of truth...' After indulging in a long homily about the 'vanities of this world', and stressing the advisibility of not seeking reward on earth which brought only sorrow in its train as well as being an obstacle 'to gaining eternal prosperity and salvation', he invited Gordon to 'abandon your present belief' and to become a convert to Islam in which case 'the friendship which pleases God and his Prophet will exist between us'. This friendly epistle, however, changed its tone towards the end. 'If after this explanation you will deliver yourself up and become a follower of the true religion, you will gain honour in this world and in the world to come, and by so doing will save yourself and all under you. Otherwise you shall perish with them and their sins and your sins will be on your head. . .'

It was an extraordinary document, full of pretention and arrogance, but with an underlying genuine note which makes one feel that the Mahdi must have considered that his 'appeal to reason' had every chance of success. And as if to add persuasion to his arguments, the letter was accompanied by a parcel and a brief note.

The parcel contained a patched Dervish smock, and the note ran —

> 'From the servant of his Lord, Mohammed el Mahdi ibn Abdulla to Gordon.
> In the name of God. On reading my answer to your letter you will understand me. Herewith a suit of clothes consisting of *jibbeh,* cloak, turban, belt and rosary. This is the clothing of those who have given up this world and who look to the world to come for everlasting happiness in Paradise. If you truly desire to come to God and live a Godly life, you must at once wear this dress and come out to accept your everlasting good fortune.'

Gordon had the letter read and the parcel opened in front of all the local government officials. He knew that if for one moment it were suspected that he was prepared to listen to the proposals from the Mahdi, or even to discuss them, it would be taken as a fatal sign of weakness. He listened icily to the translator, and when the parcel was opened on the floor, pushed it contemptuously aside with his foot before composing a reply which he ordered to be read aloud not only to the messengers but to the assembled officials.

'From Gordon Pasha to Mohammed Ahmed.

I have received the letter sent by your three messengers and I understand all their contents, but I cannot have any more communication with you.'

As the messengers left, he turned to Colonel Stewart, remarking 'I am now formally at war with the Mahdi.'

Since he had no intention of leaving Khartoum, a siege was inevitable. He envisaged it soberly but without undue pessimism — 'We have lots of food for five or six months' he wrote to Augusta 'They will not fight us directly, but try to starve us out. Our Lord's promise is not for the fulfilment of earthly wishes and therefore if things come to ruin here He is still faithful and is carrying out His great work of divine wisdom. What I have to do is to submit my will to His own, however bitter may be the events which happen to me.'

Although he could no longer deceive himself with the thought that the Mahdi's power was vastly exaggerated, he carried on outwardly as though no real menace existed. He forced the local arsenal to work nearly twenty-four hours a day turning out small arms ammunition. He designed a model for a river steamer, then had two built raising the strength of his flotilla to twelve. A system of food rationing, and especially of *dhoora* (millet), the staple Sudanese diet, was started. He even dabbled in finance, printing paper notes which, he said, would be redeemable in six months.

While busy with this mass of administrative details, he received a sharp reminder of how little he could rely on the fighting spirit of the garrison troops. Small bands of tribesmen had been noticed patrolling the desert in the vicinity of the city walls, sometimes coming within rifle range and firing a few desultory shots at the ramparts or men working on the land approach defences. Four companies were sent out to teach the tribesmen a lesson, but as soon as the Egyptian soldiers realised that their opponents had every intention of fighting, they turned and ran for the shelter of the walls.

Gordon felt that he had no choice in the matter. His men must be made to fear him more than they feared the Mahdi, or all was already lost. The two officers who had led the sortie were court-martialled, condemned for treachery, and shot. Though convinced that he had done the right thing, Gordon was profoundly depressed, and later referred to the sentence as 'judicial murder'.

By the end of April, Frank Power was describing Khartoum as a 'tower of silence in a vulture's world'. When news did leak through, it was almost invariably bad. Particularly grim for the defenders of the capital was the information that Graham's force was to stand by in Suakin to embark for India, a blow followed by the defeat in parliament of a conservative motion that 'Gordon must not be abandoned', and 'a relief force organized with the least possible delay'.

In the meantime Baring, whom Gordon unjustly accused of inefficiency and indifference, was making every effort to persuade Mr. Gladstone to change his mind, trying to impress on him that the situation was extremely grave, and not at all 'in hand' as one of Gordon's telegrams suggested. He could make no headway against the Prime Minister's stubborn anti-imperialism. An eventual reply requested that the British Government be kept up to date regarding developments in the situation and be advised 'as to the force necessary to secure his (Gordon's) removal, its armament, character, route for access to Khartoum and time of operation; that we do not propose to supply him with Turkish or other forces for the purpose of undertaking military expeditions, such being beyond the scope of the commission he holds, and at variance with his pacific policy, which was the purpose of his mission to the Sudan; that if with this he continues at

Khartoum, he should state to us the cause and intention with which he so continues. . .'

One does not know whether this communication would have had any effect on Gordon, but due to breakdowns, sabotage, and dangers en route it did not reach him till the end of July; and by then evacuation was almost beyond the bounds of possibility. In any case another more urgent message despatched on May 17 urging 'removal of himself and all Egyptians' met with the same fate. Even had it been received it would probably have been too late to act on its instructions, for on May 26, the Mahdi, freed from the threat of being attacked in the rear by Graham, made his first major move to complete the encirclement of Khartoum by capturing Berber. As a warning to those who still hesitated in supporting Allah's earthly representative, the town's inhabitants were slaughtered indiscriminately. One of the very few spared was Gordon's agent, an Italian named Cuzzi, who owed his life to the fact that he agreed to become a Moslem and adopt Dervish costume, thus earning for himself Gordon's undying contempt.

The fall of Berber meant that Khartoum's only connection with the outside world was by the river, running the gauntlet of Dervish fire from both banks, or even more dangerously by uncharted desert tracks. The fate of Khartoum appeared to be sealed. This was certainly the Mahdi's opinion who, hoping that Gordon would be sensible and realise that resistance was hopeless, sent another call to surrender this time by the hand of Cuzzi.

The Italian arrived in Khartoum in late June. Gordon refused to see him. He was quite incapable of understanding how any man could renounce his faith simply to go on living. He agreed to read the letter, but replied via another messenger — 'Giuseppe Cuzzi brought me letters yesterday in which you call on me to surrender, and do you expect that I, who am a Christian, should set the example? If you have letters to send me again, do not send a European but one of your own people.'

Colonel Stewart managed to have a word with the unhappy Cuzzi, but did not dare disclose the fact. What he learnt was far from reassuring. Cuzzi spoke gloomily of the Mahdi's 'overwhelming forces' and predicted that Khartoum would only be able to hold out a very short time if at all.

On receipt of this second refusal to see sense, the Mahdi ordered one of the ablest of his military leaders, Abu Girgeh, to invest Khartoum from the land side, and without risking a full scale assault, to keep the garrison under continual harassment. At the same time another force was to dig in on the Blue Nile's north bank so as to close the river to supply boats.

Gordon was perfectly happy for the siege to become a reality. It was the sort of situation guaranteed to bring out the best in him. Though telegraphic communication with the outside world was no longer possible, a complicated but efficient internal communication system was installed. Mines made of dynamite-filled water cans were interspersed with fresh barbed wire entanglements. Tuti Island which split the Blue Nile into two channels, was also mined, while a new fort was thrown up by press-ganged local labour at Buri to the north east of the city. Omdurman Fort, on the opposite bank, and commanding the confluence of the two Niles, was strengthed by further minefields.

A few days after Cuzzi had returned to the Mahdi, the advance party of Abu Girgeh's detachment appeared outside the walls. From then on the ramparts, and in particular the palace, and the men in the defensive line guarding the land approach, were under continuous fire. In spite of this and the fact that shells from the guns captured at the time of the Hicks disaster fell at regular intervals into the streets, morale did not suffer an immediate collapse as the Mahdi had foreseen. The 'judicial murders' had had the desired effect. In addition Gordon had found time to put his men through intensive battle training. Poor as was the material at his disposal, he had been able to instil some semblance of martial spirit into the rank and file, and make a selection of a handful of officers in whom he could have some confidence. Never had he shown so much energy or such ferocious determination not to be cowed by circumstances which would have been the despair of any other man.

Frank Power was amazed that Gordon was able to limit his sleep to a couple of hours in the heat of the afternoon, but he also gave an insight into the effect that so much concentrated effort was having on his character. He was no longer a 'lovable' man. He had become a martinet and unapproachable. He still professed to 'love' not only all those with whom he worked, but every man, woman, and child within the city walls, but in his new mood this 'love' became less and less apparent. The least mistake was severely reprimanded, the smallest misdemeanour severely punished. 'The people shrank from him in fear, his staff scarcely dared speak to him, his visitors trembled so much that they could not light the cigarettes he offered them.'

Once the net had closed, Gordon's greatest worry was his supply line. The constant fire from the land approach was no more than a nuisance. The presence of the well-entrenched Dervishes on the Blue Nile making the passage of slow-moving boats with their cargoes of grain and meat on the hoof a most hazardous affair, was, on the other hand, a most serious menace to survival. They had to be dislodged whatever the cost. Gordon entrusted the operation to one of the officers he had selected himself, an Egyptian, Mohammed Ali. It was a total success, a tribute to Gordon's genius in the handling of others. The rebels were cleared out of their positions. Few escaped, while Mohammed Ali's losses were relatively small. Temporarily demoralised, Abu Girgeh made no attempt to reoccupy his trenches.

However, in spite of the jubilation in Khartoum, Frank Power was under no illusions about the future. Only a few days after Mohammed Ali's sortie, he was writing 'We can at best hold out two months longer. The Arabs have strong forts with cannon along the river . . . when our provisions are eaten we must fall, nor is there any chance with the soldiers we have, and the great crowds of women and children, of our being able to cut our way through the Arabs. . .' He noted also that already the price of food had gone up 3,000 per cent.

The same day that the Blue Nile was re-opened for supply boats, the two messages from London which have been mentioned, arrived. Their only effect was to still further exacerbate Gordon's frayed nerves. He replied at great length. The fact that no relief had arrived, he insisted, had made him appear a liar; a wild statement since the relief column he promised had been a pure figment of his imagination. He also attacked the government for its short-sighted policy regarding Zubehr, and begged that the matter be reconsidered. As for his immediate intention, it was to march on Berber and raze the town to the ground. To the second message as to why he was still in Khartoum and what were the best evacuation routes, he grumbled 'You ask me to state cause and intention in staying in Khartoum knowing the government means to abandon the Sudan; and in answer I say I stay in Khartoum because the Arabs have shut us up and will not let us out . . . As for routes, I have told you that the one from Wadi Halfa along the right bank of the Nile to Berber is the best and, had not Berber fallen, would have been a picnic. But I fear it is too late. . .'

He chose to ignore the fact that although he had arrived in Khartoum in late February he had refused consistently to make any attempt to withdraw the garrison for the three months during which time, as he himself said, withdrawal would have been a 'picnic'.

In his first reply the statement that he intended to recapture Berber had been made on the spur of the moment.

Yet on due reflection it dawned on him that such a move was his last chance of saving the Khartoum garrison at the eleventh hour. He could not at this stage risk leaving the capital open to a surprise onslaught, even to lead so vital an expedition, but in view of the clear cut success of July 29, he hoped that Mohammed Ali would prove equal to the task.

Gordon had always stressed that the best training for battle was actual combat, and superiority complex a major victory-winning factor. With this in mind, Mohammed Ali was ordered to make a number of sorties in the early part of August. In each one sharp defeats were inflicted on the Dervishes, particularly when one of their camps at Halfaya was surprised and destroyed. Shortly afterwards a move was made against a force headed by Sheik el Obeid, one of the Mahdi's most devoted leaders exercising a great influence over the tribes in the neighbourhood of Khartoum. Mohammed Ali left the shelter of the city ramparts at the head of a thousand men, the pick of the garrison. In a brief battle el Obeid was routed. It was in the hour of victory, however, that the Egyptian made a fatal mistake which effectively sealed Khartoum's fate.

Gordon had always warned against the danger of moving too far inland beyond the effective range of the guns of the river steamers who invariably served as the artillery element for each of the operations. But Mohammed Ali, intoxicated by the sight of his fleeing enemies set off in a mad pursuit. Twenty miles in the desert, the pursuers were ambushed in thick scrub. Mohammed Ali was one of the first to be killed. Not one man of the thousand survived.

Gordon was appalled when news of the disaster reached him. Not only would he have to give up the idea of clearing Berber of the enemy, but in future he would not dare, with such a depleted force, risk a sortie to loosen the Mahdi's stranglehold on the Blue Nile approaches. To make matters worse, he learned that, buoyed up by this unexpected triumph, the Mahdi intended to increase the force investing

Khartoum and to move up recently acquired Krupp guns to batter the defences. In addition the inhabitants of outlying villages who had been encouraged by Mohammed Ali's success to trade with the capital, were now falling over themselves to bring their produce to the Mahdi's encampment and reiterate their devotion to his cause.

With deep gloom pervading the city, the Italian Cuzzi arrived before the gates with a third call to surrender. Gordon had not changed his mind. He would have no dealings with an apostate whatever his mission, and in any case, however desperate the situation, the thought of surrender never entered his mind. Cuzzi returned empty handed; without even a negative reply. But by then Gordon recognized his false optimism. He knew that his presence alone could not work a miracle. The one, the only, chance of saving Khartoum lay in the appearance of a relief column.

Since the line was permanently cut at Berber, no telegrams could be sent. The last hope, Gordon saw clearly, was for someone who had been with him, seen and experienced the dangers, and could speak with authority as to the exact situation, to return to Cairo and plead the Sudan's cause in person. Colonel Stewart was obviously the man for the job, and with him should go Herbin, the French Consul and Frank Power, civilians who in any case should not be victims of a military blunder.

Stewart was loaded with documents; the cypher key which Gordon felt should on no account fall into Dervish hands, full details regarding the garrison, its strength, equipment, ammunition statement, an exact list of supplies remaining, and a long letter to Baring. A letter full of reproaches, not only political but personal, containing such remarks as — 'While you are eating, drinking, resting on good beds we are watching by day and by night. . . I have now sent Colonel Stewart because you have been silent all this while and neglected us, and lost time without doing any good. If troops are sent the rebellion will cease. . .send troops as we have asked without any delay. . .'

All three men were unwilling to leave, particularly Colonel Stewart who was afraid he would be accused of running away in the face of the enemy, but Gordon was adamant. There was no other way. He begged both Power and Herbin to exercise all the influence they possessed to break down the obstinate refusal in official circles to face up to reality.

The departure took place on September 9. The three men travelled together on board the steamer *Abbas*, escorted by two smaller steamers, the *Safieh* and the *Mansura*. As a precaution against the cataracts proving unnegotiable, two sailing boats were towed by the *Abbas*.

The little convoy was fired on below Metemma, but to everyone's astonishment steamed past Berber unheeded. This good fortune was so unexpected that Colonel Stewart decided that since all danger was past the two escorting steamers could be sent back to Khartoum where their guns were likely to be needed for the defence, and at the same time, so as to increase the *Abbas's* speed, to cut loose the two sailing boats.

After parting company with the *Sufieh* and the *Mansura*, the *Abbas* continued to make excellent progress. The fifth cataract was negotiated without difficulty. But in spite of their remarkable good luck, Colonel Stewart was impatient. He kept urging the skipper to inspire his stokers to still greater efforts. It would have been better if he had not interfered. At Abu Hamed the Nile curves in a wide sweep to the West and divides into two channels. Steaming at full speed into the wrong one, the *Abbas* became firmly wedged on a shoal of rocks before the error in navigation could be corrected.

If even one of the sailing boats had been retained for just such an emergency, it would not have been so serious. As it was there seemed to be no alternative but to launch the dinghy and face the prospect of a long row. The three men settled into the small boat, Colonel Stewart at the oars. To begin with there was no one in sight, but they had not gone far when a man waving a white flag hailed them from the west bank. Stewart pulled in towards him. The man claimed to be a loyal subject of the Khedive and great admirer of the British. He would be delighted, he said, if they would accompany him to his village, to put camels and a guide at their disposal, and supply them with an escort as far as Dongola. There was no valid reason for suspecting him, especially as it was thought that the region was well north of the Mahdi's influence. The boat was tied up and the three Europeans followed the man they thought was their bene-factor to a village. They were shown into a hut where they waited — or so they thought — for their guide to conclude bargaining over the price that would be charged them for camels, guide and escort, when suddenly a group of Dervishes came storming in. Taken completely by surprise, only Stewart was capable of putting up a token resistance. The Dervishes were not taking prisoners. No live voice could now plead the necessity of a relief column! Equally serious was the fact that the Khartoum cypher, together with full secret details about the garrison had fallen into the Mahdi's hands.

Back in Khartoum, Gordon was convinced that his fate hung on the efficacy of Colonel Stewart's eloquence. The Mahdi's new weapons, the Krupp guns, had effectively cancelled out the slight advantage in fire power which his own floating batteries had given him. His 'flagship' the *Bordein* displayed a two foot diameter hole in her home-made armour plating. No more supply ships dared to attempt to run the gauntlet of the well served Dervish guns.

But towards the end of September when — though he did not know it — Colonel Stewart and his two companions were already dead, a messenger slipped through the Dervish ring with the news that a relief column, led by Lord Wolseley, was on its way. The letter, dated 20 September, had been written by a Major Kitchener, installed at Dongola to act as liaison officer with Khartoum; the same Kitchener who eleven years later, a General, was to command the expedition to avenge Gordon's death, smash for ever the Dervish military power at the battle of Omdurman, and hoist the Union Jack from the Khartoum palace flagstaff.

This was just the news Gordon had been waiting for so anxiously. Armed with it, proof that he had not lied, he set about trying to restore civilian morale. Streets were plastered with posters of British and Sudanese soldiers. The remaining twelve guns fired a salute of three rounds from each gun, as though the first redcoat had already appeared on the desert horizon. A long, not always strictly accurate, proclamation was issued, in which Gordon claimed the entire responsibility for the city's salvation employing the royal 'we' — 'On our arrival at Khartoum, on account of pity for you and in order not to let your country be destroyed, we communicated with the Khedive of Egypt concerning the· importance and inexpediency of abandoning it, whereupon orders for abandoning the Sudan were cancelled...therefore sufficient troops were appointed and indeed have reached Dongola and started in three divisions...They will soon be in Khartoum, be therefore fully assured as to your selves, your families and all your possessions...'

The word 'soon' as regards the expected arrival of Wolseley's army was more than an 'exaggeration'. By the end of September the only troops in Dongola were some 250 mounted infantry. The main body had only just reached Aswan, the best part of 500 miles to the north.

Nevertheless it was this heartening news that he and his garrison had not been thrown to the wolves which mitigated Gordon's distress when a messenger from the Mahdi informed him that Stewart, Power and Herbin had been killed. There could be no doubt as to its veracity. The message contained extracts from the letters and documents Stewart had been carrying. As usual, the Mahdi ended on a sermon-like note

'As to your expecting reinforcements, reliance for succour on other than God — that will bring you nothing but destruction. There is no refuge but in God and in obedience to His command and that of his Prophet and his Mahdi. . .' There followed yet another call to surrender, to which Gordon replied — 'I am here like iron. It is impossible for me to have any more words with Mohammed Ahmed: only lead. . .'

Gordon may have hoped that the Mahdi would not delay his attack too long. In his new-found optimism, he could envisage the situation where the bulk of the Dervish army raging vainly round Khartoum's impregnable walls would be taken in the rear by Wolseley's redcoats, and, thus caught between two fires, wiped out.

Nevertheless he spent hours brooding over the question whether or not he were responsible for Colonel Stewart's death, summing up 'If *Abbas* was captured by treachery, then I am not to blame . . . if they were attacked and overpowered then I am to blame, for I ought to have foreseen the chance and prevented their going. . .' As for Colonel Stewart 'He was a man who never thought of danger. . .a brave, just, upright gentleman. Can one say more?'

The relief of Khartoum had been sanctioned only after a tough battle in Parliament. Mr. Gladstone was not a man who changed his mind easily. For the day, he was a confirmed anti-imperialist, his dominating principle where foreign affairs were concerned to keep Britain out of what he termed 'colonial adventures'. But members of the House, including a number of liberals, were unwilling to abandon a man sent by them to his present post of danger. Even if Gordon were an eccentric, his life was still their responsibility. Should anything happen to him, they would have to contend not only with their own guilty consciences, but bitter attacks from the conservative opposition, and loss of support from the country at the coming elections.

There was another factor tipping the scales in Gordon's

favour. The Queen was, despite his lack of special graces and his unwillingness to appear at Court, one of Gordon's most fervent admirers. She did not hesitate to tell Lord Hartington, Secretary of State for War, that since his government had placed Gordon in such a perilous position, it was his duty to save him. She was not prepared to listen to Hartington's assurances that Khartoum could never be taken by storm. She had read all Baring's despatches most carefully, and declared that Gordon must not be left in the lurch 'if not for humanity's sake, for the honour of the Government and Nation'.

In a thoroughly belligerent mood, Gladstone told the House that the situation was well in hand, and that the opposition was trying to make capital out of 'irresponsible' reports in the press rather than relying on official statements from the departments concerned. His oratory won the day. The question was dropped; but only for a very short time.

The press returned to the attack, working up a near public hysteria. Many of the articles assumed an abusive or alarmist tone. One stated that Gordon was actually dead, but the news being officially withheld; another that he was a prisoner and had turned Moslem. Stead, editor of the *Pall Mall Gazette* was rumoured to have visited Brussels to offer the Sudan to King Leopold if he would march from the Congo to Gordon's relief. A band of 'British Sportsmen' offered to form an expeditionary force armed only with their sporting guns, and shoot their way from Suakin to the Sudanese capital.

The Queen again wrote to her obstinate Prime Minister, while Lord Wolseley was in constant touch with Lord Hartington imploring 'immediate action' and making it quite clear that he did not want to share the responsibility of leaving Charlie Gordon to his fate. Hartington, won over, responded whole-heartedly to the appeal. He told Gladstone that if nothing were done he would resign and make public his reasons for so doing. Faced with rebellion within his cabinet, Gladstone capitulated. Astute politician, he realised that if he did not do so the government might well fall.

On August 5, he himself put the motion to the House that 'a sum not exceeding £300,000 be granted to Her Majesty to undertake operations for the relief of General Gordon should they become necessary, and to make certain preparation in respect thereof. . .' Very few voices were raised in opposition.

Just over a month later, September 9, Lord Wolseley landed in Egypt to take command of the expeditionary force on its relief march of well over a thousand miles. Unfortunately for Gordon and the inhabitants of Khartoum, a vote in Parliament was one thing, getting the ponderous military machine of the day turning over so as to implement the vote was another.

To begin with weeks were wasted considering which of the only two approaches to the objective — by sea to Suakin, across the desert to Berber, thence up river to Khartoum, or the longer alternative of following the Nile's course from the start — should be adopted, before the technical difficulties involved in the former obliged the planners to decide on the Nile route. And with the decision came awareness of the appalling obstacles to be overcome not so much from enemy opposition, but from the logistic and medical points of view.

The distance to be covered was enormous; nearer fifteen hundred than a thousand miles separated Cairo from Khartoum. Marching the whole way was out of the question. It was hoped to utilize steamers for large stretches even though it meant battling upstream against the strong Nile current. When the river was no longer navigable, though many would have to continue on foot, it was foreseen that the principal means of locomotion for both men and supplies would be the camel. The original estimate of the numbers needed was 1,200, but by the time the expedition was fully under way, a host of close on 8,000 of these grotesque looking, evil-tempered, 'ships of the desert' was lurching across the shadeless wastes. The extra number called for was due to the fact that it had not been realised that not only would they be carrying men, ammunition, rations, fodder for the cavalry horses, but fodder for themselves!

The heat was blistering. Most of the British soldiers had never known anything hotter than a south coast summer afternoon. To the misery and exhaustion caused them by nature, the wretched men were stifled by their uniforms. Tropical kit was unknown. Even khaki drill, the uniform adopted by the Indian army, was frowned upon despite the Duke of Cambridge's opinion that it was 'the only thing for troops in action.' The men of the Royal Irish Regiment, the Royal Sussex, the East Surreys, the Berkshires, were issued with 'blue serge frocks, blue serge trousers (sic) and grey flannel shirts'.

Fighting against such handicaps, progress was bound to take on something of the traditional snail's pace, yet Lord Wolseley dared not travel light, adopting the principle of the 'flying column'. His whole approach to the problem was dominated by the solemn warnings that there must be no repetition of the Hicks tragedy. As one writer noted 'Defeat would imperil Egypt with all the British capital there invested, and it would in England provoke a major political crisis while seriously affecting prestige abroad. Even the balance of power in Europe might be affected. There must not be another Hicks. . .'

9

The Martyr

Calculating from the point of view of a man who had always broken records for marches across deserts, over mountains, and through jungles, Gordon was grossly over-optimistic in his estimate of the expeditionary force's probable time of arrival on the scene. He guessed that Wolseley would not drive his men to the point of exhaustion, as he himself would have done had he been in the commander-in-chief's place, but he still could not envisage that weeks would be required to cover distances that he would have annihilated in a few days. And in the hope of speeding the appearance of the first elements of the longed for British soldiers, he sent four of his steamers down river to Metemma, roughly half way between Khartoum and Berber, with orders to embark the leading companies and race them back to the besieged city.

Once the steamers had disappeared from sight, there was little else he could do but sit back and wait.

After Stewart, Herbin, and Power departed on the *Abbas,*

the Austrian Consul Hansal was the only other European left in Khartoum, but Gordon, who would never allow circumstances to temper his rigid principles, still refused to have anything to do with him. For Gordon this spiritual isolation was an added hardship. It was not so much that he needed human companionship; he craved an audience, even of one man. He loved expounding his theories on life, morals, religion. But he rejected Hansal as an evil man, dominated by Satan. The Egyptian and Sudanese officers were not capable of understanding his abstruse rhetoric. As Khartoum was cut off from the rest of the world, there was little sense in continuing to send off long letters to Augusta and Mr. Barnes which only by some infrequent miracle could reach their destination. Instead, he embarked on the writing of a diary — or journal — in which he recorded not only the day's events but, at great length and with a wealth of detail, his own thoughts, observations and reflections. This journal ran into several volumes, most of which survive, and which provide a vivid picture of the siege's closing stage.

The journal shows that although he was so insistent that it was his one chance, Gordon never entertained much hope that Stewart's mission would produce positive results. Already on September 14, entries are preoccupied with 'the end'. 'I toss up in my mind whether if the place is taken, to blow up the palace and all in it, or else to be taken and, with God's help, to maintain the faith and, if necessary suffer for it (which is most probable). The blowing up of the palace is the simplest, while the other means long and weary suffering and humiliation of all sorts. I think I shall elect for the last, not from fear of death, but because the former has the taint of suicide, as it can do no good to anyone and is, in a way, taking things out of God's hands. . .'

Though he was prepared, perhaps would have been glad, to accept this form of martyrdom, he had no wish to share his secret thoughts with the British public, or for it to be imagined that the relief expedition was being organized simply to extricate him from danger. This is evident from furious scribbling in the journal after receiving Major Kitchener's letters — 'I altogether *decline* the imputation that the projected expedition has come to *relieve me*. It has come to save *national honour* in extricating the garrison etc . . . I am not the *rescued lamb* and I will not be. .'

Whatever his private doubts, fears, and strange desire, Gordon proved himself a first class actor the last few months of his life. Never for a moment did he allow the men of the garrison or the people of Khartoum to suspect that he was other than totally confident that the city would hold and relief would come.

When the Mahdi appeared in person with all his retinue to set up his tent before the city walls so as to be present at, and witness of, Khartoum's agony, announcing his presence by sending yet another messenger with a call to surrender, Gordon still had the spirit to send a mocking reply tinged with black humour — 'If you are the real Mahdi, dry up the Nile and come over, and I will surrender.'

The journal, however, with its constant references to the end, reveals his true frame of mind, in marked contrast with his almost debonair attitude put on for the benefit of those with whom he came in daily contact.

In addition to this admission of doom, everyone with whom he had had any dealings over the Sudan question was attacked and insulted so violently, that one has the impression that these vitriolic phrases on paper constituted a necessary outlet for overwrought emotions without which he might well have suffered a mental breakdown. Baring was always the favourite target. Gordon hated the sight, sound, and thought of him. He would never admit that Britain's representative in Cairo, though reciprocating his personal animosity, had, nevertheless, being an honest and conscientious man, done his very best to influence the British Government to come to the rescue of the Sudan.

Baring was blamed for the fall of Berber because he

'openly announced that no troops would be coming up to Berber' and had therefore 'encouraged Cuzzi into betraying Berber'. Cuzzi himself was dismissed as 'A vile traitor (like all Italians I have ever met)' — he seems to have forgotten his liking and admiration for Romolo Gessi. The British Government, he accused, were so uninterested in the Sudan that they could not distinguish between the town of el Obeid and the Sheik el Obeid. 'Her Majesty's Government' he continued 'refused to help Egypt with respect to the Sudan, refused to let Egypt help herself, and refused to let any other power help her.' He added 'No success with the present expedition can possibly enable H.M.G. to justify their policy, which was alike selfish and inhuman. . .'

Later entries showed that as the weeks went by, he suffered from increasing persecution mania. He claimed that when Kitchener heard that Khartoum was invested, he exclaimed 'Hurrah! Capital news! The Mahdi has *him* on the hip. He will make no more impertinent remarks about the Intelligence Department. . .' He also kept harking on the fact that eventually Zubehr must, as he, Gordon, had always emphasized — be officially installed as Governor-General of the Sudan. That nothing had been done about it was further proof — if indeed proof were needed — of the mental bankruptcy of all politicians — 'Zubehr's coming up when I asked for him would have saved Berber'. Sometimes his anger verged on childish petulance, as when he noted — 'I would sooner live like a Dervish with the Mahdi than go out to dinner every night in London. . .'

The journal did have a practical purpose as well. When he heard that relief was on the way, he drew up his own plans for the campaign. Had his views been adopted, based as they were on the principles of mobility and rapidity of movement, Khartoum might well have been saved. He stressed 'I would not attempt to pass the *bulk* of British forces across country, only the fighting columns to co-operate with the steamers. No artillery is needed with either force . . . then in combination with us (the garrision) clear out the rebels; the affair of a week. I cannot impress on you too much that this expedition will not encounter any enemy worth the name in the European sense of the word . . . A heavy lumbering column is nowhere in this land. Parties of forty or sixty men swiftly moving about will do more than any column. . .'

But for the statement that no artillery was necessary, and the usual obstinate refusal to recognise the Dervishes' fighting qualities, the advice was sound. But as has been seen, Lord Wolseley could not afford to take risks, nor was his traditional military thinking inclined towards the employment of unconventional units and 'flying columns.'

It was strange that Gordon should have dismissed the need for artillery as every day he was being afforded further proof of the enemy's growing fire power. Once the four steamers had set out for Metemma, his flotilla was reduced to two vessels, the *Ismailia* and the *Husseiniyeh*. They were now incapable of reducing the batteries of Krupp guns ringing the city and did no more than serve — with the palace — as targets for the Dervish gunners. Soon the *Husseiniyeh* was neutralized. Engaging in a duel with one particularly tiresome gun that had been dropping shell after shell into the middle of the most crowded areas, her steering gear was damaged so that she ran aground on a mudbank at the confluence of the Blue and White Niles. The *Ismailia*, riddled by bullets and shell splinters so that she resembled a vast sieve, wallowed low in the water for a few days, a useless hulk, then sank.

The palace, on the other hand, stood up to the ceaseless battering remarkably well. Gordon simply ignored it. Every day, like sister Anne of the Bluebeard legend, he climbed up to the flat roof to scan the horizon with his telescope — this and composing his journal were his only relaxations — while bullets cracked past his ears. But each day his prayers went unanswered. The Nile's surface remained unruffled by a steamer's bow wave. The far desert was void of life, though the immediate vicinity of the walls where the Mahdi's huge army was solidly encamped 'like a vast nomadic migration' was a teeming mass of humanity, families and camp followers almost outnumbering the fighting men.

It was a miracle that he was never actually hit, for as usual, he made no attempt to take cover. In fact the more bullets whined overhead, or smashed into the walls, the more shells screamed through the hot air or exploded nearby, the better he was pleased. It was again a matter of logistics. The Mahdi had no basic ammunition supplies. The rounds now being fired derived from the booty captured when Hick's column had been destroyed. A spy had informed Gordon that, in fact, the Mahdi had a bare 800,000 rounds left, while the garrison still had a good two million and the arsenal was turning out a further 40,000 weekly.

What did worry him was the food situation. Rationing was strictly enforced, and provided theft could be kept down, Gordon had reckoned reserves would last till mid-December. But even this conservative estimate showed every sign of being over optimistic. By mid-October the effects of under-nourishment were being felt. Whenever he made one of his frequent tours of the streets, he was confronted by the spectacle of ever growing numbers of squalid swollen-bellied children, men and women lying in the dust or propped up against the mud walls, too listless to get to their feet at his approach even though they recognized him as the Governor-General, normally to them a near God-like figure. The siege had been going on so long, and for so many weeks food had been so short, that the people were rapidly losing all interest — even in life itself. They no longer cared whether the city held out or fell. If it held out they would probably die of starvation; if it fell they would be slaughtered for having resisted the Mahdi; the result would be the same in the end.

Gordon understood. It roused in him a guilt complex. But for his presence, but for his orders and the discipline he was obliged to maintain, the people of Khartoum would, for the most part, have been quite willing to open the gates to the Dervishes. As it was they had trusted him, and now because of their trust they faced certain death. But if he were guilty of being the cause of their misery, he would never be guilty of deserting them.

His grief was expressed in one of the most emphatic of the journal's entries. After more unpleasant remarks about his whipping boy, Baring — 'If a boy at Eton or Harrow acted towards his fellows in a similar way, I *think* he would be kicked, and *I am sure* he would deserve it. I know of no sort of parallel to all this in history except it be David with Uriah the Hittite. . .'. he wrote 'I declare positively and once for all that I will not leave the Sudan until everyone who wants to go down is given a chance to do so . . . therefore if any emissary or letter comes up ordering me to come down I WILL NOT OBEY IT, BUT WILL STAY HERE AND FALL WITH THE TOWN AND RUN ALL RISKS!'

Shortly after this, and a rapid visit to the food stores, from which he calculated that in six weeks there would be nothing left, was the entry — 'if they do not come before November 30, the game is up and Rule Britannia!' But on the 3rd of November for a brief moment he was deluded into the belief that his prayers had been answered.

Suddenly a steamer came in sight, running the gauntlet of Dervish fire from both banks, yet apparently undamaged. As she came nearer he realised that it was his old flotilla flagship, the *Bordein*. He was certain as she tied up that at least a company of British soldiers would come down the gangway. To his bitter disappointment there were no troops aboard, and his hopes were still further dashed when the skipper handed him a letter from Major Kitchener, saying that Wolseley, now only at Wadi Halfa, 'expected' to start from Dongola 'on or about 1 November'.

Thirty five days was the minimum, Gordon reckoned, that the force would need to cover the distance from Dongola, and faced with the cold reality, he very much doubted if he would be able to continue the resistance for so long. He thought of the shortage of grain, of the apathy of the people, growing physical weakness due to reduced rations, affecting not only civilians but the troops manning the defences, and wondered why the Mahdi hesitated to launch the all-out attack which, he now felt, he would be powerless to beat off.

The reason, though Gordon had no idea of this, was that the Mahdi was a prey to the same doubts that had assailed him after Sir Gerald Graham's victories over Osman Digna. While he took care to keep alive the legend that being God-sent he could do no wrong and that his enemies must wither away before him, he was too shrewd not to recognize the stark fact that the most fanatical bravery on the part of spear and sword wielding tribesmen, was useless against a tenth of their number of well trained, disciplined regulars armed with modern rifles. This basic truth was continually being brought home to him by one of his unofficial staff, the Austrian Rudolf Karl von Slatin, ex-Governor of Darfur, who had been forced to surrender to the Mahdi when the Dervishes overran the province and who, like Cuzzi, had allowed himself to become converted to Islam to save his life.

The Mahdi, who was a better judge of men than Gordon, formed a high opinion of Slatin's power to sum up a situation, and of his knowledge of and insight into world affairs beyond the Sudan's confines. He kept him constantly by his side as private adviser on all matters concerning Europe and Europeans. News had reached the Mahdi that Wolseley's force was on its way, and that it was composed of British regulars. There was, therefore, no hope of repeating the victory in which he had annihiliated Hicks's jaded, battle-shy Egyptians.

Apart from undernourishment, a weapon on which the Mahdi was banking, the health of those within Khartoum's walls was surprisingly good. But in his own overcrowded camp, with its appallingly unhygienic conditions, fevers and dysentery raged. Nor did he feel he had still the same iron control over his followers as in the early halcyon days. It could not be said that any had shown signs of rebelliousness; it was just that he was not always as readily obeyed as before. Later when reports came through of bloody defeats at the hands of the redcoats in the first clashes far down river, proving the overwhelming man for man superiority of the British soldiers, his misgivings increased to such a degree that he was seriously considering breaking off the siege. He was afraid that even if in the end he did storm Khartoum, he might find that he himself was shut up in the city which he had been besieging, the situation reversed, and unable to break out through the British ring. For a long time, in fact, Gordon's optimistic proclamations were far nearer the truth than he himself guessed. Another thing Gordon failed to realise was that von Slatin — whom he now despised, just as he did Cuzzi, for having changed his religion to preserve his skin — still loved and admired the man who held him in such contempt, and was doing his best to discourage the Mahdi from ordering a general assault by playing on fears of Wolseley's approaching columns in the hope of persuading him to strike camp and so avoid a major clash which, so Slatin assured him, could only prove disastrous.

There is a probable, but not wholly confirmed, story that one of Gordon's messengers was picked up and found to be carrying a letter which was handed over immediately to Slatin for translation. The Austrian found that it spoke in such grim terms of the garrison's dire plight, that it was likely to encourage the Mahdi to attack without delay. Risking his life, Slatin pretended he could not understand it because it was 'in French cypher language', and asked if he might be allowed to get in touch with the Austrian Consul Hansal, who it will be remembered had refused to leave the city, even though Gordon would have nothing to do with him. The Mahdi gave his permission and ordered Slatin to write yet another call to surrender of his own dictation ending, 'Know, O thou enemy of God, there is no escape for thee from death at our hands and death by lack of food.' This was just what Slatin had hoped for, as it gave him the chance to slip in a personal note of his own in which he implored Gordon to accept the offer of his services, to allow him to change sides and, if necessary, lay down his life in the defence of Khartoum. Gordon was completely unmoved. He rejected the call to surrender and ignored Slatin's pathetic appeal.

If Gordon had been able to communicate more freely with Lord Wolseley, and in the early days had not written with such obstinate, unjustified optimism about the situation in general, despite War Office admonition that caution must dominate every move, the Expeditionary Force's progress might not have been so leisurely. As it was the wheels of the Staff machine turned with incredible slowness. A whole month was allowed to drag by at Wadi Halfa discussing transport problems, and Wolseley himself did not reach Dongola till early November.

Under the impression that time was on his side, the Commander-in-Chief planned to advance in a solid mass, rather than adopt the 'flying column' tactics advised by Gordon. Then there was trouble with the steamers which could have been avoided. Those built in England were late arriving, and then found too frail for the purpose, on top of which coal supplies were totally inadequate and had to be brought up to the required tonnage before a move could be contemplated.

Once under way, no one, least of all Lord Wolseley, seemed to be in any real hurry. The leisurely advance was maintained all through November and most of December, until on the 30th of the latter month, an alarming report was received which left no doubt as to the gravity of Khartoum's plight. The gist of the message was that though the enemy could only succeed by 'starving us out', the food situation was not merely 'acute but critical'. Wolseley was begged to 'come quickly' but warned, rather surprisingly, 'Do not scatter your troops; the enemy are numerous.' He was also strongly advised to secure Berber firmly before continuing the advance.

Wolseley knew Gordon well enough to take the report extremely seriously. But he was faced with a dilemma. He could hardly 'come quickly' with his main forces and their vast cohort of transport animals, yet to send a lightly armed mobile column might be to invite disaster against a 'numerous enemy'. In the end, perhaps inevitably, he arrived at a compromise. Keeping his main body intact for the attack on Berber, he detailed the Camel Corps, the Naval Brigade, and a battalion of the Royal Sussex Regiment, under the command of Sir Herbert Stewart (no relation to the murdered Colonel Stewart) to advance overland with all possible speed to Metemma where the infantry would be embarked on steamers for the last stage to Khartoum. But even this infinitely more mobile contingent was slowed down by the need to protect the wells against Dervish scorched earth policy, so that the dash for Metemma did not get off to a start before 13 January.

Three days later, nearing the Abu Klea wells, Sir Herbert Stewart's little force which only totalled 1,600 men and 2,400 camels and horses, sighted a horde of Dervishes, judged to be at least ten thousand strong.

A few shots were exchanged before the sun set. The night was calm. The British were too exhausted after the long day's trek across the open desert to attempt to repeat the manoeuvre in the dark followed by a first light attack which had proved so successful against Arabi Pasha at Tel-el-Kebir, but just after dawn formed a hollow square, certain that the Dervishes would need no special encouragement to attack.

The famous British infantry square had been the rock on which the tide of Napoleonic victories had broken in the Peninsula, and finally at Waterloo. In 1885 it would have been a hopelessly outdated formation in Europe, but was still supremely effective when dealing with such enemies as the

Dervishes or the Zulus.

At Abu Klea, however, Sir Herbert Stewart was faced with the problem of advancing rather than waiting stationary to receive the enemy charge. After the battle one of the naval brigade officers commented 'A square moving forward had to keep exactly the same pace on all its sides if great gaps were not to appear making one side straggle or bulge. The manoeuvre was never easy, and at Abu Klea it was made more difficult by the need to take some camels into the centre of the square to carry the guns and bring back the wounded. Their presence made the square bulge ominously this way and that, but particularly to the rear. .'

There was something of Crécy or Agincourt about the battle which followed.

The outnumbered British, relying on their controlled fire much as the British yeomen had relied on their bows, calmly awaited the enemy onrush led by mounted Emirs, the equivalent of the French Chivalry. The first volleys fired at close range brought down hundreds, but the Dervishes, worked up into a frenzy of fanaticism, defying death, actually broke into the square, a feat unique in history. Even Kellerman's massed heavy cavalry had failed to smash into one of Wellington's squares despite the fact that the British infantry fire power, armed with the clumsy muzzle-loading musket, could not compare with that of the Naval Brigade and the Royal Sussex modern Lee Enfields.

Strangely enough it was the presence of the camels, looked upon till then as such a nuisance, that really saved the day. 'The defenders at the rear and left flanks' wrote the same officer 'fell back upon the wall of camels. For a couple of minutes a desperate hand-to-hand struggle went on between the attackers and the thin defence line, with the Arabs (sic) hacking, heaving, hamstringing, and yelling like a crowd of black devils on a ground literally piled up with dead and dying. But now some of the rear rank at the front of the square turned and began to fire into the mêlée. This burst of organized fire had a devastating effect on the Arabs. They had faced withering fire to reach the square, had broken into it, and now they were faced by organized volleys again. It was too much for them. They wavered, turned, and retreated, not in total flight, but slowly and sullenly. . .'

Not one of those who had actually broken through got away. When the attack was finally beaten off, there were over a thousand dead piled up inside, while British casualties numbered only seventy-four, amongst them the British second in command, Colonel Burnaby, whose loss was deeply felt. He was one of the great characters of the day; an individual like Gordon, but more of the cavalier than the roundhead, a noted dare-devil adventurer known for his famous 'ride to Khiva'. His question 'Is Mr Gladstone's government to live, or Gordon to die?', had roused the country. Determined that wherever there was fighting to be done, he must take part in it, he had pulled every known string to be included in Lord Wolseley's expeditionary force. A giant of a man, he had fought like a devil during the battle. Even after being stabbed in the throat by a Dervish spear, he carried on and 'laid about him with a sabre before collapsing. His death was particularly mourned by the men in the ranks.' A lieutenant remembered seeing a young soldier kneeling beside his dead body, in tears, and saying — 'Oh sir! Here is the bravest man in England and no one to help him.'

Their losses did not dismay the Dervishes. Though they had the good sense not to risk another attack, they sniped at and harassed the column the whole way to Metemma, slowing the march to such an extent that two days were taken to cover the ten miles from Abu Klea to the river. These tactics proved far more trying for Stewart's men than the brief fury of the pitched battle by the wells, and when the column was actually within sight of the Nile, fortune suddenly came down on the side of the Dervishes. In the course of a sharp encounter, Sir Herbert Stewart was hit and mortally wounded.

Automatically, the next senior officer, Sir Charles Wilson, since Burnaby had died of the wound in his throat, took over command. Sir Charles was an excellent staff officer, but not a bold leader. All his soldiering career had been spent at a desk. This was the first time he had ever had an active command, and from the British point of view and in particular that of Khartoum's defenders, the moment could not have been more unfortunate. Obsessed by the need for caution, he wasted precious time overhauling the steamers' engines when all his efforts should have been concentrated on getting his men to Khartoum, even if the steamers broke down on arrival. His dilatoriness was all the more to blame since Gordon's journals, which made the extreme urgency of the relieving forces' arrival most brutally clear, had been handed to him as soon as he reached Metemma. In the journal he could read from an entry as far back as December 13 (1884) that if no help came within ten days 'the town will fall'. While other notes, completely contradicting the advice of Lord Wolseley not to 'scatter his forces' stated 'All that is necessary is for fifty of the Expeditionary Force to get on board a steamer and let their presence be felt, this is not asking much but it must happen at once, or it will as usual be too late. . .'. Yet in spite of these warnings, it was not until January 24 — they had reached Gubat just below Metemma on January 21 — that the two steamers *Bordein* and *Talatawein* started on the five day journey to Khartoum.

At the end of November, Gordon made a last attempt to put heart into the people by issuing further proclamations regarding the nearness of the British relief force. It had no effect. He had cried 'wolf' too often. He was not altogether suprised by the lack of reaction and was himself more than ever resigned to the fate which he now saw was inevitable. It was in early December that he had ordered the *Bordein* back to Metemma with the last volume of his journal. Its final entry read — 'NOW MARK THIS, if the expeditionary force does not come in ten days, *the town may fall;* and I have done my best for the honour of our country. Good bye!' And there was a last batch of letters to various friends, including of course Augusta and Mr. Barnes, and a last official report to the Chief of Staff, Sudan Expeditionary Force, which was matter-of-fact, and categoric in its statement that the garrison's situation was 'extremely critical, almost desperate'. It was a sentiment echoed in the letter to Augusta — 'This may be the last letter you will receive from me, for we are on our last legs owing to the delay of the expedition. However, God rules all and as He will rule to His glory and our welfare, may His will be done ... I am quite happy thank God and like Lawrence (Sir Henry Lawrence defender of Lucknow in the Indian Mutiny) I have tried to do my duty.'

December dragged on. The Mahdi's army encircled the town, though apart from stepping up the bombardment made no offensive move. But by the beginning of January the threat of starvation had become a reality. People were not just hungry, they were dying in the streets and being left unburied for the vultures to pick their bones. Till then the city had been free of disease, but now dysentery was rife; at any moment typhus was expected to break out. Like the citizens of Paris in 1871, Khartoum's inhabitants looked upon rats as a luxury. All horses, donkeys, dogs, and cats, had long since been killed and eaten.

The situation was even worse in Omdurman, principal fortress and strong point of the capital's defence system. There was no food, and ammunition reserves were almost exhausted. When, on January 5, Gordon was told that the last round had been fired, very reluctantly he gave permission for the garrison commander to surrender. Omdurman's fall was the virtual end of the siege. It meant that from the fortress's ramparts, Dervish riflemen could fire direct into Khartoum, their guns pound the city walls with near total immunity.

Yet the Mahdi still could not make up his mind to order

153

the final assault. He sent a last letter which, on the surface, is difficult to understand. He held every trump card in his hand, yet was almost pleading with his beaten enemy to stop fighting and avoid further bloodshed. One can only draw the conclusion that in Gordon he divined a fellow spirit, a fellow visionary, like himself a chosen of God, whom he was unwilling to destroy.

The letter was addressed to Gordon Pasha 'May God protect him. We have written to you to go back to your country. I repeat to you the words of God. "Do not destroy yourselves. God is merciful unto you." ' Then came an extraordinary offer — 'I understand the English are willing to ransome you alone from us for £20,000. If you agree to join us it will be a blessing to you. But if you wish to rejoin the English, we will send you back to them without asking for so much as a farthing. . .'

If not for himself, it was a tempting offer for the sake of the population whose lives were in Gordon's hands. He has been blamed for not accepting, and by his refusal sacrificing the people to his selfish death wish. But this was probably not his only reason for his rejection of what, on paper, was a more than generous offer. It is likely that he had no confidence in the Mahdi's promises, and again he was still forcing himself to believe that at any moment the spearhead of the Expeditionary Force would appear on the horizon. Although the roof vigils were now doubly dangerous with Dervish marksmen installed the length of Omdurman's ramparts, he spent even longer than before with his telescope trained on the Nile, hope being reborn when, after news of Abu Klea was brought to the Mahdi's camp, he saw women tearing their hair and heard their high pitched wailing as the names of those killed in the battle were made known.

A wealthy Sudanese business man who had frequent dealings with Gordon, and who survived the Dervish occupation, later described the havoc wrought by months of strain on Gordon's character — 'The people stood aside scowling at this maniac of a white man who was throwing their lives away in his pride. He had come to this town a young man, hard but cheerful; now they saw an old man, white haired, white moustached, face lined. His wrath was terrible, unaccountable; at any moment he might burst out on them, kicking, shouting, punishing. Some of the notables protested he should make peace with the Mahdi. He threw them into prison. He made the round of the defences hour after hour watching with hawk-eyes for the man nodding at his post, the man who had not repaired an Arab breach, the man whispering sedition to another, the men cowering from the bullets. They were beaten, they were thrown in prison. . .'

Towards the end, Gordon had renewed twinges of conscience. He would not tolerate any hint of surrender on the part of the garrison while there was still a round left in the magazines or a single man still capable of squeezing a trigger. But at last he took pity on the civilian population. Those who wished to do so, he announced, were free to leave and go over to the enemy, adding that he would address a personal letter to the Mahdi asking him to be merciful. When the city's gates were opened, nearly twenty thousand moved out to the Dervish encampment. Gordon was pleased to see them go. Their departure meant a few more crumbs for those who remained.

After the news of Abu Klea penetrated to Khartoum, it was obvious both to Gordon and the notables that the eleven months old siege was approaching its climax. The Mahdi had to make up his mind; to attack or depart.

Left to himself, the Mahdi would probably have taken Slatin's cautious advice and retreated, but in his hestitant mood, instead of making a personal decision as he had done invariably in the past, he called a meeting of his Khalifas to whom he declared that Allah had spoken to him in a dream telling him that he must leave Khartoum and return to his own conquered province of Kardofan, otherwise disaster would overtake not only him but his followers. It was a sign of his declining influence that anyone dared question his decisions, especially when he vowed that he was merely expressing Allah's will.

The Mahdi's uncle, a tough man of the desert, Mohammed Abd el Krim, led the opposition arguing that the garrison was in no condition to resist a determined assault, and that though Gordon was without doubt a remarkable man, he certainly did not possess magic powers. Furthermore the Abu Klea disaster made it of vital importance that there be no delay. Every moment was precious. The attack must be ordered within the next few hours. Abd el Krim's solid common sense swayed the Khalifas. Possibly, also, the Mahdi felt that he no longer had the influence to over-ride a majority vote, in any case he agreed to act upon the advice of the council rather than that of Allah. The assault, he decreed finally, would be launched before dawn of January 26. On one matter, however, he was adamant. Gordon was a man of God, even though not a Moslem. He must be taken alive *and unharmed*. Any man hurting him would be accused of contravening the Mahdi's law. At the same time he gave his blessing for the ruthless slaughter of every single man of the garrison, Turk, Egyptian, Negro, traitor Sudanese, without discrimination.

Within Khartoum, the last three days were stormy.

No one could understand why, if it were true that the Dervishes had been heavily defeated at Abu Klea, there was no sign of the victors. Gordon had promised that the British would be in Khartoum 'in a day or two' so often before, that most of the notable and senior officers of the garrison were led to suspect that the Abu Klea victory was nothing but a figment of the imagination designed to spur flagging morale. The garrison commander, Faragh Pasha, became so convinced that this was the case that he demanded a personal interview with the Governor-General, which was granted on January

23, twó days before the Mahdi's decisive conference with his Khalifas.

Faragh came straight to the point. It was obvious, he said, that there would be no relief. If indeed reports of the Abu Klea battle were true, then the British commander must have decided, as Sir Gerald Graham had done the previous year, that there was to be no further advance. The garrison was too weakened by privations to offer serious resistance. He urged Gordon to do the only sensible thing under the circumstances, and raise the white flag.

Gordon lost his temper. He told Faragh he was a fool to believe the enemy when the garrison commander produced a letter purporting to come from the Mahdi and stating that not a man would be harmed if surrender were immediate. To begin with, steamers packed with British soldiers would be sighted any moment, and in addition the Mahdi was not a man who had ever showed mercy to those who had thwarted him. The *only* hope was to fight on. Faragh remained obdurate. The discussion grew heated. In a fit of uncontrollable rage, Gordon slapped Faragh across the face.

Next day Gordon summoned the city notables. They begged him to make up his quarrel with Faragh and also to give serious consideration to the Mahdi's surrender proposal. He would not even talk about Faragh; a treacherous coward. As to surrender, he said furiously, the only reason the Mahdi had made the offer was because he knew the British would be on him at any moment. It was an offer from weakness which would be treated with the contempt it merited. He admitted that the garrison troops were on the verge of collapse; but it was no longer a question of days before relief came, it was a question of hours, a very few hours!

The last person to see Gordon alive and talk with him after the notables had been dismissed was Bordeini Bey, a rich Khartoum merchant.

'I found him sitting on a divan' Bordeini recalled some years later 'and as I came in, he pulled off his tarbush and flung it from him saying "What more can I say? I have nothing more to say. The people will no more believe me. I have told them over and over again that help would be here, but it has never come, and now they must see that I tell them lies".

'He was afraid that the people would see despair in his face and so made his last promise through an intermediary that in 24 hours the English would arrive. He said that he expected an attack that night and ordered every male from eight years to old men to be forced if necessary to the defences. Yet, he added, if the commandant insisted, he was at liberty to open the gates and "let all join the rebels."

'He ended the interview by saying "If this my last promise fails, I can do nothing more. Go and collect all the people you can on the lines and make a good stand. Now leave me to smoke these cigarettes." There were two full boxes of cigarettes on the table.

'It was a gloomy day that last day in Khartoum; hundreds lay dead and dying in the streets from starvation, and there were none to bury them. At length the night came and, as I afterwards learnt, Gordon Pasha sat up writing till midnight then lay down to sleep. . .'

Gordon was correct in his prediction that the attack would be for that night. The most talented of the Mahdi's military commanders Wad el-Nejumi was chosen to lead the assault planned for half past three in the morning, with the main body crossing the moat by a natural mud bridge formed by a sharp drop in the river level. The vanguard met with even less opposition than expected. Gordon no longer had the power to galvanise his men, or even to terrorise them. They were dropping at their posts with fatigue and inanition. Before it was fully realised that the attack had begun, the Dervishes had broken through the defenders and were swarming into the city, so that those who had tried to fight back soon found themselves being fired on from the rear.

Resistance collapsed. Those who had the strength to run fled, pursued by the screaming Dervishes; others, trying pathetically to hide, were stabbed as they cringed in dark corners pleading for mercy.

A group yelling 'To the Palace!' stormed into the palace gardens slaughtering the guards on the gates.

Trampling down flowers, breaking through hedges, they reached the foot of an outside staircase leading up a verandah. Suddenly the leaders stopped so abruptly that they were almost knocked down by those behind charging into them.

To everyone's amazement, Gordon was standing at the head of the stairs, immaculate in his white uniform, his scarlet tarbush on his head, his hand resting unconcernedly on the hilt of the sheathed sword hanging from his left side. There was not a trace of fear on his features. He stood looking at the men who had come to kill him, his expression a mixture of contempt and irritation.

He had been sleeping soundly when the tumult from the streets woke him, bringing home the fact that the Dervishes were through the defences; that the siege was in fact over. Without hurrying, he washed and shaved, dressed himself in his parade uniform with as much care as if he were to attend a levée then walked out unconcernedly to face the shrieking mob and death.

For a few moments there was the rigidity, the silence, of a *tableau vivant*.

It was broken by the Dervish leader. Forgetting, or ignoring, the Mahdi's strict injunction that Gordon was to be taken alive and unharmed, he gave a shout of 'Accursed one! Your time has come!' and hurled his spear. The point caught Gordon full in the chest, spinning him on his heels. As he fell, the others were on him hacking and stabbing. The leader then grabbed a sword, struck off the head and had it sent back to the Mahdi. Gordon Pasha's headless body lay at the foot of the stairs for most of the day, young Dervish warriors coming from time to time to blood their spears in his mutilated corpse. It was not till evening that, with several others, it was thrown into a well.

When the bloody head was brought to the Mahdi, he could not believe that his orders had been so deliberately disobeyed. Thinking there must be some mistake, he told the bearer to take the head to von Slatin for identification. The Austrian has left an account of the gruesome incident. He was in despair at the time, suffering from intense depression brought on by his failure to dissuade the Mahdi from launching the attack he knew all along could not fail.

'The sun was rising red over the horizon' he wrote 'Soon shouts of rejoicing and victory were heard in the distance, and my guards ran off to find out the news. In a few minutes they were back again excitedly relating how Khartoum had been taken by storm. I crawled out of my tent and scanned the camp; a great crowd had collected before the quarters of the Mahdi and the Khalifas; then there was movement in the direction of my tent. In front marched three black soldiers; one named Shatta, formerly belonging to Ahmed Bey Dafalla's slave bodyguard, carried in his hands a bloody cloth in which something was wrapped up, and behind him followed a crowd of people weeping. The slaves had now approached my tent and stood before me with insulting gestures. Shatta undid the cloth and showed me the head of Gordon.

'The blood rushed to my head and my heart seemed to stop beating, but with a tremendous effort of self-control I gazed, silently, at this ghastly spectacle. His blue eyes were half opened; the mouth was perfectly natural; the hair of his head and his short whiskers were almost quite white.

' "Is not this the head of the unbeliever?" said Shatta holding the head before me.

' "What of it?" I said quietly "A brave soldier who fell at his post. Happy is he to have fallen; his sufferings are over." '

Those of Khartoum who remained with Gordon till the

end paid a very high price for their loyalty. During the first day, over four thousand, including Hansal, the Austrian Consul, were butchered. Turks, among them Faragh Pasha, the man who had urged Gordon to surrender and been insulted for his pains, were tortured before being put to death. Old women were murdered, the young ones taken as slaves. Next day, tired of killing, the Dervishes plundered and looted. If a man were suspected of having hidden his personal belongings, or failed to give up all he possessed willingly, he was beaten almost to death. The Palace, after being sacked, was burnt.

Two days later, the steamers *Bordein* and *Talatwein* sighted Khartoum. Sir Charles Wilson saw smoke rising over the city, and as they drew closer, Dervish guns opened up. Though several shells fell very close, they pushed on almost as far as the confluence of the White and Blue Niles. There could be no mistake. The Palace was a smouldering ruin over which no flag floated. Khartoum had fallen. They were too late! Sir Charles Wilson saw no point in sending his handful of men, outnumbered by something in the neighbourhood of three hundred to one, to certain annihilation. Reluctantly he gave the order to head back down stream.

To have landed would have been suicidal and served no purpose. On the other hand a bombardment by the steamers' guns, would perhaps have been a gesture, a show of force which would have acted to some extent as a face-saver. The Dervishes expected it. It is said that they could not believe 'that the much vaunted soldiers of England, the victors of Tel-el-Kebir, had not stayed to exact some retribution for the killing of their fellow countryman.'

When news of the Khartoum tragedy reached England on February 11, the whole country turned against the Gladstone Government. The Prime Minister's chief assailant was none other than Queen Victoria herself who told him categorically that she held him as directly responsible for Gordon's death. To Augusta she sent a personal letter in which she spoke of 'Your dear, noble, heroic brother who served his country and his Queen so heroically, with a self sacrifice so edifying to the world . . . I do feel so deeply the *stain* left upon England for your dear brother's cruel but heroic fate. . .'

Till Khartoum, Gladstone had been known in England as the G.O.M. — the Grand Old Man — but now the intials were reversed to read M.O.G. — Murderer of Gordon.

Condolences poured in from all over the world: from the Khedive, Nubar Pasha, Li Hung Chang, even the Emperor of China. Lord Wolseley went as far as to say that the world 'would never see his (Gordon's) like again.' The day funeral services were held at St Paul's Cathedral and Westminster Abbey was declared a public holiday, while the Government, anxious to try to make good the damage to the Whig cause, voted a sum of £20,000 to the Gordon family. This belated generosity could not save them. At the next general elections, the Whigs were swept out of office to be replaced by a Tory régime headed by Lord Salisbury.

Today, ninety years after his death, when summing up calmly Gordon's merits and faults, one can see that the latter were many and varied: a tendency to twist, even disobey, orders, an obstinacy which at times could only be described as pig-headed, bigotry, impoliteness, an inability to control a violent temper. His death at Khartoum, the slaughter of its citizens still within the walls when the Dervishes overran the defences, was totally unnecessary. He himself wished to die. It did not occur to him, till too late, that others might not share his wish. Yet with all these shortcomings, the embryo of genius was within him.

In his day he was a symbol; the Stainless Knight, fearless in the face of the enemy, dauntless in the face of adversity. A typical hero figure of the late Victorian era, he was worshipped by the English public; as one writer put it, 'for his incorruptibility, his cool cheek, his truly English devotion to every cause but that of England. . .in short for his sheer impossibility!'